Praise for *D*

Barry Thain - *Clinical Hypnotist Mindsci Clinic*

Deeper and Deeper claims to be "a complete instruction course" in stage hypnosis, and actually is. Of course, and as it makes clear, no book can gift you the natural talent to hold an audience let alone entertain it. But if you have the personality and professionalism to carry it off, you probably wouldn't ever need another book on stage hypnotism to make a career of it. It is just what you would expect such a volume to be, covering everything from setting up the venue to turning the lights out as you leave. The techniques necessary for volunteer selection, rapid inductions, deepenings and entertainment routines are all dealt with clearly and concisely, and Jon includes his 'super suggestion' which every therapist should have in their armoury.

Deeper and Deeper is very matter of fact. It is written with great weight and authority because it is the distillation of decades of real life experience, devoid of speculation or theory. Everything Jon writes can be done, has been done. And it doesn't take much imagination to recognize the practical applications for the consulting room.

Grant Boddington - *editor Hypnotes*

Jonathan Chase's book 'Deeper and Deeper' is a very 'nuts & bolts' approach to Stage Hypnosis a 'Complete Instruction Course' in a book; and should be appreciated by those with experience, as well as by newcomers to the profession.

I linked instantly to Jonathan's wit and directness in 'Deeper and Deeper' and read parts of the book several times. If you get only one piece of useful information from any book then it's well worth the time and money. From this book, I'm sure most Stage Hypnotists (whatever their level of ability or experience) will get a great deal more!

I especially liked Jonathan's obvious concern for the safety and well-being of his volunteers as well as his attention to the 'behind the scenes professionalism' of a successful Stage Hypnotist.

I recommend this book very highly and look forward to any subsequent writings from Jonathan.

Bryan Dean - *Magic Talk*

For some very peculiar reason these days there are a lot of books and seminars on Stage Hypnosis. Some of these courses run into the thousands of dollars, but are they worth it?

Perhaps. Well, here, in a wonderful new book by England's hypnotist, Jonathan Chase, is a great way to start performing the art of Stage Hypnosis.

Jon begins by giving you a fine intro into what hypnosis is, how it is recognized, etc. Also about the "dangers" of Stage Hypnotism. (I learned one safety technique here that was worth the whole price of the book.)

Then he teaches you not a long drawn-out but very quick induction where your subjects are hypnotized by the time they are on stage. This is a newer technique unlike what is known in the United States. He teaches you how to structure your show and how to put it together with props, etc. There is only a basic outline for the show Pre-Talk (no scripts is included, but he shows you how to create one yourself). He includes ten pages of routine ideas which should help you along. Highly recommended for all magi-cians and related arts.

DEEPER AND DEEPER
The secrets of stage hypnosis

Jonathan Chase

"The Dream Pilot"

published by
The Academy of Hypnotic Arts Ltd.
PO Box 186 . Falmouth . Cornwall . TR11 4WB
www.hypnoarts.com

First printed edition 2005
Printed and bound in Great Britain by Antony Rowe Ltd.
ISBN Number: 0-9547098-1-0

For my sons
Ben and James,
who are my reasons

Contents

Acknowledgements

I have a few people to thank:

Jay Ceetan Marni and Robin Colville for getting me started. Jimmy Carlo for nothing really but if I don't he'll cry. Jane Bregazzi for her patience and hard work. Barry Thain for being a great sparring partner. And not least the thousands of people who have trusted me enough to allow me to gain my experience by playing with their creativity.

Author Photograph Kay Foster
Show and cover photograph Jane Bregazzi

Thanks Jon

ABOUT THE AUTHOR

Jonathan, a self-confessed showbiz junkie who's worked in the 'biz' as a roadie, stage manager, sound engineer, tour manager and of course an 'act' in his own right, became intrigued by hypnosis after receiving therapy to alleviate the effects of a genetic neuromuscular condition, a condition that makes his achievements even more remarkable.

He studied much after this and found he had a natural ability for the use of the hypnotic art, even being persuaded to begin a remedial consultancy. His love of the 'biz' though, was a draw, and the fact that he couldn't sing, dance or act, originated 'The Dream Pilot'. With total mesmerism (I use the word loosely) he spent a couple of years watching all the hypnosis acts he could see and was taught the Stage Hypnosis game by two well known entertainers: Jay [Cetan Marni] Ruffley a Red Indian knife throwing Ninja hypnotism act, and comedian and backstage hypnotist Robin Colville from the Grumbleweeds.

He found it easy to combine both private consultations for remedial and performance purposes with entertainment hypnosis and fast became known for his innate prowess with all aspects of what he calls "the beautiful art".

In this time Jonathan has built a wealth of experience and has performed in more places than is possible to list, here are but a few:

Weekend Live (Central Television), *Beacon Radio* (Wolverhampton '91) performing the first 4 hour comedy hypnosis show live on air, *Piccadilly Radio* (Manchester) performing the second. *West End* (London), *Limelight Club* (Shaftsbury Avenue), *Theatre Royal* (Stoke-on-Trent), *Pavilion Theatre* (Devon: Two Record breaking summer seasons), *Prince of Wales Theatre* (Staffordshire), Palazzo *Pescatori Restaurant Theatre* (Malta), *N.E.C.* (Birmingham), *UK Forces* (UK & Europe). He is an established entertainment for many corporate clients including; G.P.O., Club 18-30, B.B.C., Royal Air Force, H.M. Forces, Trust House Forte, Ringways Ford, Port Vale Football Club, and has appeared at literally hundreds of exhibitions, functions and presentations, from small bars upwards.

As well as all this he has managed to find time to co-write and direct a comedy musical *'Laughter & Tears'*, premiered at the Prince of Wales Theatre 1998 and to qualify as a Certified Master Hypnotist (UK) and as a Master of Mind Integration Therapy (USA).

In 1991 he made hypnosis history performing the first live four-hour long comedy hypnosis show on radio, using invited volunteers from the general public and by broadcasting a twelve show series of past-life regressions live on air for Wolverhampton's *Beacon Radio*, with an estimated audience of over 250,000. He also writes song lyrics, comedy sketches, reads Tarot cards and teaches stage and remedial hypnosis and is often approached by strange people asking for the price of a cup of coffee. Must be exhausting!

It is estimated that he has hypnotised well over 70,000 people on and off stage – he thinks it is closer to a third of a million – although I have it that he didn't count. Now he feels it is time to pass his knowledge from doing it, the right and the wrong way, onto others.

When I read this book – having no experience of hypnosis – my first words were 'is that it, it can't be that simple?' In fact hypnosis is simple and with the right practical learning experience, hypnosis is accessible to all.

Jonathan writes candidly and honestly about a subject that he knows inside and out and isn't dressed up with unnecessary technicalities. This book 'does what it says on the tin'. You will find it to be an easy learning process that is enjoyable as much as you find it useful.

Jane Bregazzi

WELCOME

Okay, so why another book on Hypnosis? Because this book is not just about hypnosis, but Stage Hypnosis which for many people is their first contact point with the hypnotic arts. Although all hypnosis is hypnosis no matter where it is performed on or off stage, there are obviously elements such as performance and presence which are peculiar to the entertainment world.

This is the second version of this book, the first being published as an electronic book on the Internet. We've decided however to produce a printed version because of the many requests causing the death of several managed forests and to use up some recycled toilet tissues. I was also asked to add more sections about making money and the business side of things, which I've done. I'm now working on the complete stage hypnosis script CD and booklet, which word for word gives you the actual delivery and wording for every routine and induction you'll find here.

This is not just another how to do it for dummies book. If you're a dummy, forget it! Nor is it a purely technical manual. It is, in my humble opinion, the first book I have yet to see that handles the modern style, used by the best hypnotists working the stage today, written in an open and frank manner. It's not a script for a full show, although the skeleton for that is here. It won't tell you how to be a star; you'll have to figure that out yourself. It does give you the tricks of the trade but definitely does not give you the talent to entertain. Hypnosis can be learnt, talent cannot.

I have been asked on occasion, since putting the word around that I'm writing this, 'why cut your own throat?' as if I will be creating competition. For one, I am mostly concentrating on other uses of hypnosis and training now. For two, they'd have to be very good indeed to usurp my hard-earned standing in the trade. If they are that good then they will do this anyway sooner or later, so why worry?

The reasons for writing this are many fold, not least because the few other books that I've read on this particular facet of the hypnotic art are dated and / or boring and uninformative beyond belief. I won't mention names but certainly if you went out and did the suggested shows like this to a modern audience they would eat you alive – leave – or worse still ask for their money back. If the writing itself makes you yawn, just think what their actual shows must be like!

Another reason is that Stage Hypnotists hold a unique position in the entertainment world. There are so few of us, and far fewer who are actually any good. We are the ultimate specialty act; even virtually unknown performers can command fees far higher than most others. We can perform literally anywhere. I've done shows in tents, bars, theatres, cabaret clubs, and sitting rooms and even once in a swimming pool (although none of us got wet). I've performed to thousands and to a handful (and I do mean five).

However the thing that we have in common, other than what we do, is something that no other performers share; we are 'THE Hypnotist'.

To explain, let me give you this scenario. You go along to your usual club, bar, whatever, where you listen to a comic or singer or magician most Saturday evenings. Some of them are brilliant, some okay, some passably bearable and some dire. You watch the bad ones and think, 'oh well, the girl / guy last week was good,' and you keep coming back. One bad comic or singer does not make them all bad.

Perhaps because of the uniqueness of our art though, 'THE Hypnotist' does not fit this scene. For some strange reason when a person sits through a very badly presented or even failed hypnosis show, they think we are all one and the same. Most of the time they don't even remember 'THE Hypnotist's' name and even believe we are the same person. Why? Because there are so few of us. We are seen so rarely by our audiences that most seem to believe we all do the same act, which of course we don't but then in that case a singer is a singer is a singer.

Individual members of an audience may witness a hypnosis show once, maybe twice in their lives, and unless they become a hypno-holic following you from town to town or you are lucky enough to be a singing hypnotist who gets in the charts on occasion and on the television a lot, the name fades into the obscurity of their memory. What remains is the recall of seeing 'THE Hypnotist'.

Realising this helps us understand why every established act in the world, winces at the very thought of someone hitting the headlines with bad press because they screwed up big time. We are 'THE Hypnotist' and when that screw-up occurs we all get flack. 'THE

Hypnotist' can, unless we are very well prepared, be the target of every lawyer and or journalist looking for his or her own notoriety. We are in the one profession, as far as show business is concerned, that relies totally on dragging the public up to entertain their friends for us, using, what has long been held by the general public and of course the more sensationalist journalists in the media, to be a dangerous form of mind control and brainwashing.

It should make sense therefore when I say that the ultimate reason for writing this is to ensure that anyone coming into the business, after reading this, is not going to make mine and my established colleagues lives a living nightmare by causing bad publicity for 'THE Hypnotist'. If you practice, read, remember and recall, you will not screw-up. If you do, go get singing lessons.

In the following pages I am going to presume that you really want to be a Stage Hypnotist, that you can perform the mental equivalent of standing on your head on a twelve-foot spike while juggling three full-grown bull elephants and reciting the complete works of Shakespeare backwards. I am also going to assume that you have little or no stage knowledge. If you are already in the biz and find some of the contents a little obvious, don't yawn, hang in there, there's always something else to learn.

I'm going to tell you what I believe to be the underlying psychology that makes the whole thing work, and how to use that. I'm going to warn you of the pitfalls I've encountered but will not for one moment pretend that I've found them all. There's always one more.

What I will not do is blind you with science, dogma, or pretend that everything in here is purely my own idea. That would be like a comic laying claim to the mother-in-law gag. (That's been around as long as mother-in-law's and was therefore written by the first religion to come up with marriage, as a way of making us feel guilty.) I will not 'pad' the book out so that it is metaphorically thicker and therefore more value for money.

I will give you all the knowledge I believe you need in practical terms and even try to pass on what I believe you need to have in terms of style and personality, to become a Hypnotic Show person. Remember however that this is not a thesis, argument, or diatribe so if you are a psychologist or a hypnotherapist who believes that anything in here can be disproved by whatever module or school of thought you subscribe to, then you are entitled to your opinion; as I am to mine.

On a purely practical level I have done everything described in these pages and it works, and will work for anyone else that understands the how. I do have to say however that neither this, nor any book on hypnosis, is a real substitute for hands on personal training as that offered on our masterclass at the Academy of Hypnotic Arts, and as such accept no responsibility for anything you do with what you find in these pages.

Good luck with whatever you do with what you find here, and to quote a showbiz friend of mine when I told him I was going to be a stage hypnotist, 'Are you insane?'

THIS THING CALLED HYPNOSIS

My dictionary describes hypnosis as: 'A state like sleep in which the subject acts only on external suggestion; an artificially produced sleep'.

In a 'real' sense this is not entirely accurate, in fact it isn't even close. It does however describe what the average person perceives the state to be. In fact, it describes what many hypnotherapists believe the state to be, and they are also wrong.

This definition describes exactly what hypnosis is not. Hypnosis is not sleep or even relaxation and apart from the fact that, generally speaking, most people close their eyes in the state, and the fact that I and every other hypnotist uses the word sleep on stage, there is no similarity to sleep in anyway whatsoever.

Unfortunately it is we stage performers who tend to perpetuate this myth. Saying, "Sleep" is easier and far more dramatic than saying, "please return to the altered mental state where your imagination is expanded and your inhibitions are lowered". It's a darn sight quicker, and the audience expects it…and they do pay the wages.

During a hypnotic state your brain produces mostly the same waveforms as when you are wide awake. In some cases there is a slight rise in the levels of activity produced by the right side of the brain, which is generally recognised to be the imaginative centre, otherwise everything is normal. In fact you can experience hypnosis with your eyes open whilst walking and talking quite freely, ask any stage hypnotist's subject.

Also, hypnosis is not unconsciousness. Unconscious people are the world's worst conversationalists, tending to lie about and not do a lot! As the hypnotist will at least need to talk to their friends on stage, and they to the hypnotist on most occasions, being unconscious would present a few small problems to the hypnotist. In all cases of hypnosis the subjects are perfectly aware of what is being said and done. It's just that the level and quality of their awareness is focused in a different way from the norm and belongs to the psyche or subconscious mind rather than the logical conscious brain. In other words, in hypnosis our conscious logical mind is dormant and our subconscious or more accurately our psyche or 'mind' is dominant.

So if we can be fairly definite about what hypnosis is not, can we be so sure of what it is? For the purposes of this book, yes.

A few 'experts' would argue against this point but then 'experts' have been arguing the toss about everything from the existence of God to the nutritional value of a Big-Mac, for thousands of years. Hypnosis has been argued about for as long – and probably always will be. You see hypnosis is a function of mind. You cannot touch, smell, taste or feel mind, only the tool of the mind that is the brain. This being the case we can only make assumptions based on our own findings, experiments and observations. In other words an 'educated' guess, here's mine:

Hypnosis is the state of psychic (subconscious) dominance and it also describes the art of direct communication with the accepting psyche. In hypnosis this manifests itself in the unquestioning acceptance of suggestions delivered by outside means.

Many people have the impression that this is an 'idiot' state similar to some drug induced conditions: a state where your capacity to be human is reduced and you become machine-like. Then like a machine, if someone presses the right button you will spew out all the information your computer of a brain holds, or accept any old rubbish put in there, as irrevocable truth. And in the first edition of this book I stuck to the generally accepted theory that this wasn't true.

It is a fact that whether hypnotised or not, you are, and remain, completely human. While hypnotised you can be secretive or open, you can lie or simply be mistaken. You can choose to ignore, accept or reject outside suggestions, and be as obstinate or co-operative as you wish. You remain completely human. Which of course means you *can* accept any old rubbish as irrevocable truth – sometimes.

So let's look at what happens in the hypnotic state:

When hypnotised, the conscious or ego part of the brain becomes less critical, if you like, it becomes 'relaxed' and inattentive, although the level of this 'inattention' varies hugely from person to person depending on how well the state has been induced.

By less critical I mean that the part of our mind that we recognise as 'me' – our conscious – is bypassed so that thoughts and impressions reach the rest of our mind without being filtered by our critical and logical faculties. We become rather like a small child who still believes that there really are fairies at the bottom of the garden, and if mummy kisses it better, then it gets better. This is a perfectly normal state of mind which for some unknown reason someone called 'trance', and because no one has come up with a better label we will call it that too.

It appears similar to when we daydream and even when we watch TV, (although in fact the two have nothing more in common than a passing resemblance,) especially soaps – that's why billions are spent every year on television advertising at the times these shows are on, or do anything which requires little or no logical or conscious thought. But the hypnotic version is way more intense and it has focus, and the reason the ads work is repetition, not hypnosis.

Have you ever driven the same route for the thousandth time and then realised that you don't consciously remember anything of the journey? Well that isn't hypnosis either, but it is a good explanation to use when persuading people to take part. I like to call it "lies to children", because it reminds me of such wonderful phrases as "Don't sit too close to the television - your eyes will go square." "You'll have someone's eye out with that". And the good old, "Your face will stick like that when the wind turns". All rubbish and no more accurate than saying hypnosis happens in this way naturally.

Hypnosis then, is a way of communicating with our creative mind, our inner being, or psyche, which appears to be the largest, most powerful and most misunderstood part of 'us'. The part which not only regulates all of our bodily processes such as breathing, blood flow and oxygen distribution, and all the other millions of bits and pieces that take place unnoticed inside us every second. It is also the part of us which reacts to our memories, instincts, drives and passions. It is the seat of our dreams and sometimes our nightmares, the guide and guardian of our future, our past, and the store of all-mental energy and purpose. More importantly, for our purpose, it is the seat of our emotions and creativity.

Hypnosis labels a process that helps us to contact this wonderfully creative beast inside us directly, and once we've achieved that we can make changes. And when we direct the largest part of our mental potential to do what we want it to, boy can we change!

A little history is important here to allow an insight into this phenomenon. The man many consider to be the father of hypnosis as we know it, (although in one form or another it's been around as long as man), a Frenchman named Anton Mesmer told people that he could cure their ills by 'Human magnetism'. Later to be called 'Mesmerism' by someone with little or no imagination (but Saatchi and Saatchi weren't around at the time). All he did was to stick two bits of metal in a bucket of water and get the patient to hold on to the ends. Sound unbelievable? The thousands of people he cured, of everything from Gout to Hysteria, must have thought differently! The damn thing worked; so much so that towards the end of his career he had to magnetise trees and get his patients to hold hands around them, there were so many customers. Then some bright sparks from the 'Real' scientific world came along and discovered that there was in actual fact no such thing as 'Human magnetism' which made Mesmer a fraud and a pauper, and meant it was possible to walk through the two white pillars in stores and airports without setting off all the alarms.

However, not everyone was a sceptic and in 1842 a Scottish surgeon named James Braid used the self-same method of suggestion in his practice to operate on a few thousand people, with a mortality rate far below those of his fellow Doctors. Not wanting to be branded as yet another charlatan, he dropped 'mesmerism' and coined the phrase HYPNOTIC from the Greek 'Hypnos' meaning to sleep. Where the word Hypnosis comes from is not clear, Braid certainly doesn't use it in his writings so it is probably a bastardisation that occurred over time.

Braid was of course a man blessed with the skills of being able to get people to believe in the process and in him. Unfortunately, or if we take the case of Hitler perhaps fortunately, not everyone has such charisma naturally. So when a chemical form of anaesthesia was discovered – and when it was proved that anyone and everyone could use it – Doctor Braid's methods were put aside for the easy alternative.

True to say the mortality rate during surgery shot up, often caused by the new drugs. Those that did survive took longer to heal, were generally more uncomfortable and not quite so happy about things. But such minor faults can be overlooked, can't they? And anyway opiates and analgesics, which again could be administered by just about everyone and their aunt, could handle the pain and we went on to develop such wonders as Valium and Prozac to take care of feeling happy. Of course these drugs don't do that but they ensure you don't care how you feel so the end result is no unhappiness.

As for Doctor Braid, taking his nationality into account, he must have been really put out; drugs cost money and hypnosis was free! Unless of course you wanted to see what it was all about and the only way to do that was to pay for a ticket to see an operation. This rather neatly brings me back to the subject of this book....

WHAT IS STAGE HYPNOSIS?

Stage Hypnosis is the public demonstration of the effects of hypnotic suggestion on an individual, according to British law that is. There is no difference between the state seen on stage or in the office – that is if hypnosis is being used and not psychotherapy with some guided relaxation, which is what most therapists settle for. Hypnosis is just hypnosis and shouldn't be described by where it's done. We don't say office hypnosis or living room hypnosis which is where the vast majority of the rest is done. But stage hypnosis is as it says, usually performed on stage, or radio, or television or anywhere as an entertainment by a performer.

To most onlookers it is a demonstration of how minds can be controlled and forced to produce unusual reactions in poor, weak-willed and unfortunate volunteers, by one possessed of amazing insight and wonderful knowledge, (much to their amusement of course). The amazing and wonderful bit I agree with totally, but then I would, wouldn't I? Then again those same people probably believe that a sword actually passes through the arm of the magician and that the politician's promises will be kept. Bless them; they are your best audience.

Stage hypnosis however is a unique and astounding phenomena, and unlike therapeutic hypnosis the effects cannot be produced in the majority of the population all of the time. Only around twenty percent can be successfully induced into the state usually known as, for want of a better word, somnambulism quickly enough to be used on stage at any particular time... It's a mood thing. If they are in the right mood they will 'go'. And yes moods can be changed but on stage you don't always have the time. Everyone can be hypnotised given time, some take longer than others but I have yet to meet the person who can't be hypnotised.

This being in the right mood for fast induction is why virtually all Hypnosis shows start with twenty or thirty volunteers from an audience of two hundred plus, and finish with any number less than that at the end. There is of course always the exception that disproves the rule. I worked on one occasion with thirty two people in the state when the audience was just under a hundred; I've also ended up, but only in the early days, with one out of five hundred!

While in this state most of the 'subjects' will be experiencing hallucinations. If they don't, you don't have hypnosis, on stage or not. Their inhibiting functions are not entirely lost but are lowered considerably so you will see levels of apparent resistance to suggestion although this is easily bypassed. Whilst in the state of 'trance' their imaginations are expanded to the point where they can improvise and role-play as well as, and often better than, the world's most famous actors.

For the last hundred years or so hypnosis has been dogged with an image akin to witchcraft and human sacrifice, thanks mostly to the voices of derision from the youngest of 'real' sciences, psychology, and to the fictitious film character Svengali, who 'took over' people with mesmerism and got them to do a bit of stealing and murdering for him. Of course some therapists would also tell you it is thanks to us few hypnotists who use the expanded imagination of volunteers on stage to entertain, that reduce its credibility.

This is never more obvious than when accepting suggestions given by the stage hypnotist. I have seen homophobes quite happily trying to seduce members of their own sex. Introverted and normally self-conscious people, who wouldn't take their Mac off on a beach, quite happily stripping to their underwear and sometimes, although never deliberately in my shows, beyond!

Please note that I personally have never stripped a woman (hypnotised on stage that is) and have only ever gone as far as underpants with men. I do suggest you are careful here, not everyone likes the constraints of underwear, and some like it a little frillier than you'd suspect. In the case of stage hypnosis the process is a release of normally held social conventions where the subject feels free and uninhibited enough to experience the scenarios given them by the hypnotist, so please do be careful what these are.

Stage hypnosis is often a person's first experience of the art and it is still the most mistrusted, misunderstood and besieged. The horror stories are, of course, endless and for the most part without foundation.

The problem stems from the fact that the general public is kept continually and firmly in the dark about the whole thing; mostly by the hypnotists themselves, who seem to have an intense fear that if the truth is known then they will no longer have a profession. Utter rubbish! Take for instance the case of thousands of magicians whose basic 'secrets' are common knowledge for anyone interested enough to buy a child's book on conjuring.

The basis of stage and indeed ALL hypnosis may come as a shock when you look at it closely, and the importance of this cannot be under stressed – ALL hypnosis is purely the results of belief in hypnosis! Whether it happens behind closed doors or on a stage. It really is the same principal as that used in TV advertising and politics. If the observer believes that they have little biological monsters in their sweat then the soap powder sells; if they believe the best person to run a multi-million pound business which affects almost every aspect of their daily lives doesn't need any experience or knowledge of business affairs or people skills, then the dyslexic anarchist plumber becomes mayor!

NO hypnotist can force anyone to enter a hypnotic state, nor can they keep him or her there against their will…although it is possible to hypnotise without the recipient's knowledge if you are really persuasive – and it is possible to cajole and influence even an outwardly blocked mind to do things it may not do otherwise.

NO hypnotist can make anyone do anything that they do not really wish to do. No more that is, than any good con-man, or a few pints of falling down water. Some hypnotists would argue that you couldn't get anyone to perform an act that goes against their moral values and / or beliefs. However these morals and beliefs are, in most people, a very thin conscious veneer kept up for social acceptance and can often fall away with other inhibiting factors when hypnotised, just like being smashed. It's important that you understand that a person hypnotised on stage very often has no morals for the time they are with you, so moral standards are up to you.

A hypnotist on stage should be a responsible guide. They can show you how to get there and provide blueprints for your imagination to work with. But on the whole, unless the hypnotist has read this book, the results remain as unpredictable as next year's Derby winner or your first attempt at a highly collapsible soufflé. Hypnosis is an art which means anyone can do it and the only difference between you and the hypnotist is that they know how.

In actual fact the art involved in being a STAGE hypnotist is not just learning to hypnotise, anyone can do that and it really can be learnt in minutes. But to make the whole process entertaining takes talent, masochistic tendencies and a death wish; fortunately not everyone possesses a combination of all three.

So what is actually happening out on those boards?

Stage hypnosis works like this. When you are hypnotised you are less inclined to be self-conscious; rather like being drunk. When you are intoxicated, should someone suggest that it would be a bit of a laugh to pretend to be a Martian, or Elvis, or a Ballerina, or whatever, you'll probably try it – why not? It's only a giggle after all. You do try it and it gets a few laughs, so you do it some more because making people laugh is good fun. That fun is intensified by your 'intoxicated' state and so you enjoy it more and so on. If the Hypnotist is adept at helping you retain that lowered inhibition and maintaining a high degree of audience reaction, then the fun of being funny lasts as long as you stay in that state. In fact it can often be so good a feeling that you'll get people just pretending to be hypnotised, (how to spot them and deal with them later).

After the show your subconscious can put the blame firmly on the Hypnotist by apparently not allowing you to consciously remember anything that happened on stage! So you appear to your friends and family as a helpless and hapless victim and the Hypnotist takes the role of wicked villain, which of course we must be because of the ridiculous things we 'forced' you to do.

Occasionally the routines we use upset the friends or family that have come along with the volunteer, which is unreasonable when you consider that the person on stage was precisely that, a volunteer, and a willing one at that! The strange thing seems to be that if you were smashed out of your skull by an alcoholic overdose and chained yourself nude to a letterbox no one would blame the barman or the box. However the lack of reason shouldn't be a reason for your ignoring this on the odd occasion when it arises and is proof positive of how good your charm skills are as you smooth over any concerns after the show.

The important thing to remember about stage hypnosis is that done well and with responsibility and a recognition that accidents can and do happen, it is good harmless fun for the audience, volunteer, and fortunately most of the time, for the Hypnotist. It is also comparatively safe. But also remember that it is very fleeting in effect and you will have to be prepared to work hard to keep the whole thing going.

HOW TO RECOGNISE HYPNOSIS

The easiest way to see if they believe they are hypnotised is to watch their reactions to your suggestions, if they are responding as if their reality has changed without question then they are hypnotised. But we are mind and body and in most cases there are autonomic reactions to the state, some that cannot be faked, and others that the majority of people are not aware of.

Muscle flaccidity:

The muscles around the face look relaxed and the mouth opens slightly. Shoulders slump and if you've used the hand lock their hands will separate very easily if not automatically. We know they don't need this relaxation but they don't! So it does happen.

Reduced rate of breathing and / or increased depth:

Nice slow deep breaths are good. If they are snoring you've taken them too far.

Hypnotic blush:

Many people when hypnotised show patches of increased blood flow below the skin of the face and especially the neck, probably related to muscle relaxation and the associated increase in blood flow. If they are wearing too much make up or you can't really see them, then body temperature rises with the flow, and usually increases by as much as two degrees or so.

R.E.M:

Rapid eye movement, common in sleeping people whilst dreaming. In hypnosis it means that their creative mind is working full blast. In my experience these subjects tend to have the best imaginations.

They may show some, all or none of the above to greater or lesser degrees. The true test is: are they following your suggestions to the letter, instantly. If they are showing most of the tell-tale signs then you have a good subject who will stay the course. If none of them are there, then you may 'lose' them as the show goes on. They will simply stop responding to suggestion. (See hints and tips for what to do when this happens).

THE BIG SECRET

By this point it should be obvious, if it isn't then perhaps you should be planning a career in Yak farming or something. The BIG, yet simple secret of stage hypnosis is this...they believe you are THE HYPNOTIST and you can...YOU believe you are the hypnotist and you can, therefore – you can.

Remember that everything relies on the volunteers' belief systems. Stage Hypnosis works because they want it to and believe it can. Therefore once hypnotised they will behave in the way they believe to be correct for the state of mind they believe they are in.

Most people will accurately describe the antics of a hypnotised subject on stage even if they have never seen a live show. They know how it goes. This knowledge, whether gathered directly by them watching a show or by hearsay, will provide the foundations for their belief. And belief is a powerful thing. In the same way that advertising and mothers remedies work, stage hypnosis works because they know it does.

And that brings with it a responsibility for the hypnotist because if they believe you can give them a negative suggestion – then you can. Ignoring this would be stupid. We only have to look at the news to see how powerful belief can be.

WHO MAKES A GOOD STAGE HYPNOTIST?

Can you sell a freezer to an Eskimo? Then you could probably make a reasonably good hypnotist. However if you can sell one to a Polar Bear while at the same time selling a Seal the all new, but untested, Polar Bear detector then you'll make a HYPNOTIST. The two things are virtually the same. You are selling two things: 1) one of the most feared and likewise wanted experiences there is: 2) you are selling yourself.

The way you do this is entirely up to you, although I'll give you a few pointers. However you must have one important factor in your personality whatever your approach, you must believe you are the best there ever was, or will be. We are not talking an inflated ego here just absolute confidence in your abilities. If for one second you doubt yourself, the audience, by some sort of telepathy, reading your body language or perhaps being told by their spirit guides or a newspaper review, will know.

They will doubt you and disbelieve. You must not allow them the opportunity. They have to trust your skill and, unless they have seen you before or worse still seen a less than competent performer, they have to trust you based on what they see and hear before them. So from the very moment you decide to do a show, whether at a party or on a theatre stage, you must know in your heart of hearts that you cannot fail.

You must possess self-confidence. You have to believe in yourself; in your abilities and your knowledge, as people will pick up on any lack of belief on your part before a word is spoken. You must exude undying faith in yourself and I cannot stress this enough. I'm not saying that you could never successfully induce anyone without this self-assurance, but you will have one hell of a game filling the smallest stage and stay good at your job, without it.

One of my students, who shall remain nameless owing to the fact that he wouldn't pay my exorbitant fee for a mention here, once introduced me to his friends and family as 'THE HYPNOTIST, the MAIN MAN', (his capitals, not mine). He then went on to say that if he became half as good as me he would be happy. True, I am the best hypnotist that ever swung a brick with a watch painted on it at a volunteer on stage. I believe that utterly. However *he* was wrong to think that. I explained to him that as long as he thought that way he would always be average. Now, thanks to a little self therapy, he believes he is the greatest there ever was and is subsequently building a profitable reputation for himself…and one day he may be half as good as me!

You must have a gift of the 'gab'. You must be able to talk commandingly and clearly. Not being precisely understood by your subjects is one of the greatest problems you could ever have. Accents are fine providing they are not too heavy, but colloquialisms are out, (unless of course you are working in your own area but even then I wouldn't use them). People can travel some distance to see you and maybe even to join you on stage. That clarity is a must; you must be able to talk persuasively and with charm. If you could sell snow to Santa and get his Robins to crap on your thumb while eating their dinner, then you are probably persuasive enough – just. Hypnosis is the hardest sell of them all. In literally a couple of minutes you have to impart and instil ideas and compel action on them. A really good technician can do it in seconds; my personal record is twenty seconds before my first subject was under. I'll explain how, later. As soon as that action takes place, you have made your sale; the contract is signed and there is no thirty-day cooling off period. Indeed I was once approached by an executive at a trade fair in Leicester where I was performing, who told me that all he'd need was a dozen salesmen on his team with my ability for sales dialogue and he wouldn't need to throw money away on trade fairs. Thank the Gods he did need to. It was a nice little earner.

Finally you must be able to think rapidly, juggling about four or five things at once. This is no easy feat. To clarify, take a quick look at some other forms of entertainment…

A comic has to remember his gags and time them precisely; a singer has to remember the words of their songs and to wave their hands about in the appropriate manner; a magician has to remember where he put the ruddy rabbit. They all have to be aware of their audience and the latter's reaction to whatever it is they are doing. The remembering is easy. Once the song, joke or trick has been packed away in the memory the only thing to think about is his or her presentation, and where to get rabbit proof trousers.

However your job is dealing with members of the public, on stage, hypnotised. True you will have remembered your patter and suggestions, but unlike any of your fellow performers, the majority of your show cannot be rehearsed or remembered. Nor for that matter is it entirely predictable unless you know what you are doing. You not only have to think about delivery and timing; you will have to be extremely observant of the safety and reactions of your subjects; you will have to be aware of your audience and be able to adapt your routines to fit their response. Finally you must know what 'level' each of your volunteers is in and whether to deepen or raise that accordingly. It may not seem a lot but in practice you had better have outstanding adrenal glands.

I believe that the natural ability to do all this adds up to that indefinable something called talent. And talent you have or haven't got. Talent is the only part of stage hypnosis that cannot be taught in the pages of this or any other book, and will obviously mean that not everyone can be successful.

IS IT DANGEROUS?

This is the number one question 'THE Hypnotist' is asked.

Even though we are discussing STAGE hypnosis the answer is the same for any form of the discipline and art:

Yes. It can be.

Always tell your public this; you will go up in their estimation by accepting the responsibility.

The main danger however is toward the hypnotist. I know of one performer who told a three hundred-pound truck driver that he, the performer, had just trodden on the trucker's pet pixie. He neglected to tell the man that under no circumstances would he get angry or hit the hypnotist. I now know a hypnotist whose bent nose is considered quite fetching by some ladies; but was that worth the risk?

To be serious though, of course there are dangers, but most can be eradicated completely, if you are aware of them. The important point is that all of them have everything to do with you 'THE Hypnotist' and absolutely none of them have anything to do with the state of hypnosis itself.

We are dealing with people; that can throw the spanner into the most carefully designed machine. Just look at the numbers involved. Say on any given Saturday night, in clubs, pubs, nightspots and theatres, there are fifty hypnotists working in Britain. If we hazard a guess at an average eight people hypnotised per performer, that’s four hundred. If each hypnotist does only three shows a week, that's one thousand two hundred hypnotised subjects a week, four thousand eight hundred a month, fifty-seven thousand six hundred a year. In the numbers game sooner or later someone somewhere will slip and twist an ankle or bruise a knee. Maybe even fall off stage and break something. Murphy’s Law says it has to happen. It has on occasion happened. In fact once it happened to me personally! I fell awkwardly at a show, causing a reticular fracture of my right femur.

Why would a volunteer have fallen from the stage? It’s happened on more than one occasion but I have personally never ‘lost’ one. It happens usually because their eyes are closed. This can only happen if the hypnotist is an idiot and not paying attention, or as in some cases of whiplash, the volunteer is well known to insurance claims investigators. Never allow movement on stage unless the subject’s eyes are open and you make sure you have yours open as well. Okay so get the same number of people as are annually hypnotised to walk along two hundred yards of uneven footpath and the accident rate is liable to go up by comparison, rather than down, but they are not your people on your stage.

You must realise that if you are diligent and attentive, watching your volunteers’ every move, then the likelihood of any untoward occurrences can be minimised and should be eradicated altogether. So the only danger in stage Hypnosis is physical and only appears if the Hypnotist is unobservant and careless.

As for any psychological danger it does exist. Especially if the volunteer believes it to exist! That's why we must enlighten everyone about the process and make sure we tidy up well after the show. Obviously it is possible to instill a phobia as easily as one can be removed but I don't think there is enough focus on these events on stage to install anything permanent. In saying that, always make sure with a simple phrase that "Everything will be returned to normal".

You may not be convinced. It may be that you have read or heard about people being assaulted while hypnotised and that this was done without the person's knowledge. If that were the case then how did you get to read about it at all? Surely if the hypnotist were that good, they would be very careful to wipe any memory of the assault from their victim's mind? There have been reports of this happening but all of these cases have involved a hypnotherapist whose 'victim' if such they are, was in a very unbalanced and emotional state. All of these incidents have supposedly happened behind closed doors in therapy situations, with no witness. We stage performers, however, usually have a couple of hundred witnesses watching our every move, so tend not to assault anyone.

Another question that you will be asked time and time again is, "Can I get stuck in hypnosis?" and the stock answer is:

Not unless you happen to be a beautiful princess who likes apples and has a wicked stepmother. Even then a kiss from a passing handsome prince works wonders.

Let's look at an imaginary scenario. You are on stage with a hypnotist who is unwell – really unwell. She or he leads you into a very deep hypnotic state and then they notice a sharp pain in their chest. Before they can get you back to total awareness they clutch their chest, fall over and hit the floor stone dead! If you were to believe some people this would leave you in hypnosis for the rest of your life because only that hypnotist and only their voice could bring you back out again. So you'd be stuck there...forever!

What would actually happen of course is that when they hit the floor with a bump, the noise they make would ring every alarm bell you hold in your mind and snap you back to your normal state instantly. Or, if you have a particularly elegant operator who floats across the void in comparative silence, even your subdued conscious would begin to wonder after a few minutes as to why they are no longer talking to you and why there seems to be a lot of running around going on. Your instincts would bring you back to your fully aware state, if nothing else but to complain that you are wasting time on a silent hypnotist.

Even in an extreme case where you are in the deepest of states and find nothing unusual in the lack of hypnotist and couldn't care less, you would do one of two things. Get bored with the whole thing and snap out, or fall into a natural state of sleep and wake up in a couple of hours if someone didn't wake you beforehand. It's only common sense that should anything happen then you will do one or the other. Actually it would probably be the other. A lot of people I have talked to complain of falling asleep while listening to hypnotic tapes and so they never hear the end.

I'd like to cover here the rumours of things happening after the volunteer has left the stage. Some of these rumours are true. Some people have been found to be reacting to suggestions hours after being on stage. There are a few reasons for this.

The first could be that the hypnotist, being an idiot, forgot to tell them that the show was finished. This unfortunately still occasionally happens. Unless the hypnotist makes a point of spending the last few minutes of their show tidying up and making sure that the volunteers know it's all over.

The second reason is slightly more complicated and works like this, going back to the fact that being on stage makes the subject very popular. Sometimes a volunteer when on stage enjoyed the popularity and the attention it brought so much that, as far as they were concerned, it would be a good idea to carry the whole thing on for a while: just to stay popular. I have also known this to happen as a deliberate act to make me look foolish. I found the best way to handle things here was to explain that the person in question could not have been hypnotised at all. If they had then they would obviously have accepted the suggestion to act normally afterward, which I actually give them at the beginning of every show.

The third is that the person could very well have such a stressful or simply rotten life that being hypnotised is preferable to their reality and staying there seems like a very good idea. This is once again simple to deal with in your wake-up procedure.

I opened this section with a little anecdote, but it does show where the main danger in stage hypnosis lies…to the hypnotists themselves. And even if we are extremely careful in this age of 'stuff it, let's sue,' we can still suffer a great deal from pure coincidence. I would guess that more than one or two alcohol and curry induced vomiting spells, or flu-induced headaches have been blamed on the hapless hypnotist.

Goes like this. The careful hypnotist has double-checked that none of his subjects have any gastric problems and has given Fred an onion and told him it's an apple. Fred has probably eaten raw onion on sandwiches and in salads for most of his life with no ill effects. Simply holding the beast and munching will have no aftermath other than bad breath.

Now Fred, being a creature of habit, leaves the club and goes for his regular Saturday night bum-burning curry on top of sixteen pints of falling-over water – taken after the show of course. Now this Saturday the chef at the local restaurant or take-away has decided to take a chance on that piece of meat that looked a little grey-green when it came out of the freezer. Fred eats, drinks some more to wash it down, goes home and goes to bed.

Three hours later he is kneeling before the porcelain retch-alter shouting for Hewie. Of course, our Fred is not going to blame the curry. He's been eating the **same curry** for ten years. He will not blame the beer because Fred can drink a horse under the table...so it can't be that, oh no. He blames the unusual not the usual.

Having never been hypnotised before, well that's unusual enough, and being given a very fresh and completely harmless vegetable to eat, in one simple moment bang goes the performer's good name.

There is absolutely nothing you can do about this other than simply to not give your subjects anything to eat or drink, although that really makes no difference because you will be blamed for anything that happens within the next 48 hours anyway. So be careful and on occasion hope for some luck.

There is one other danger to the hypnotist that I feel must be mentioned, it's what I'd like to call, 'The Svengali Syndrome'.

If you don't know, Svengali was a character in an old film of the same name. This guy was portrayed as a hypnotist with amazing and evil powers over others' minds. He would first bend the will of his powerless victims and then force them to commit awful crimes on his behalf, including murder; while he publicly made sure he had an appropriate alibi. He had complete control; could make them do literally everything and anything. The danger here to you as a hypnotist is not only the obvious one of some peoples' view of hypnosis still being coloured by this load of rubbish, even years after it hit the screen, but this…If you are good, especially if you find that you are very good, then you may begin to believe that you can make anyone do anything. You become in your own mind a Svengali. Be careful of this.

A large amount of confidence and even ego is undoubtedly an asset for a stage hypnotist, self-delusions are not. I have met people who are so careless because of this that they often become their own reason for a downfall.

Also it should be obvious by now that it is possible to persuade most people to perform any act that they would readily perform with a reduced sense of conscience.

The point is their conscience IS lowered if not removed altogether and you have no idea what these people are capable of. They may be socially compliant on the outside but lots of people thought Harold Shipman was a caring doctor rather than a mass murderer akin to Hitler but not everyone at the German death camps were evil ghouls and devils. Remember it's only conscience that stop us being what we are deep down – animals.

There is a small but significantly vocal school of thought that says hypnosis does not exist and is therefore only social compliance or going along with things. This is true. Hypnosis doesn't have the reality of a rock, but then neither does Christianity, Islam, Nationalism nor any other belief system. Hypnosis exists enough to change peoples beliefs and therefore their reality. To believe this isn't so is stupid and dangerous, just as stupid as believing a loaded gun won't harm if you don't pull the trigger, causing to you leave the safety catch off.

I would guess that these people think this way because they have never been hypnotised and experienced the phenomena of being unable to move an arm that they know is there but have become disassociated from.

The fact is that you may be very good but you are not very God and it's only a fool who would try to judge where people might go, so don't go there.

However no one I have met and hypnotised has completely lost the boundaries of what they consider to be acceptable social behaviour, although this clearly differs from individual to individual. You are not forcing anyone to do anything. You cannot order them to perform in such a way that goes against their most deeply held instincts.

You may be very good, but you are not very God.

Maintain an open and honest self-view of your capabilities at all times and you will retain a healthy self-regard.

MAKING IT SAFE

Knowing that you will be working with people and understanding that the human body breaks very easily; here are a few pointers to ensure that your show is as safe as it can possibly be.

Be sober and think slowly – act fast…and make it a **personal** thing between you and those people who will be earning your wages with you.

Always personally check the chairs and stage you will be using. I have seen chairs held together with masking tape and string 'if, of the folding variety - don't use them,' or stages with potholes that would put some Maltese roads to shame. Remember that you have no idea who will be joining you on your performance area. You have no idea how they will be dressed. Some women still wear high-heeled shoes. A stiletto will find a small hole very easily and a broken ankle brings things to an abrupt halt.

Check and double check everything, and I do mean everything. I once worked a club where, without stretching, I could easily reach up and touch the low-slung lighting gantry. No discernible problem you may think but I am six feet one inch tall and could easily have one or two people on stage that may be taller. Now if I did a routine such as a ballet dancer where you would expect arms to be thrown upwards and even the odd enthusiastic leap, then remember that after being on for half an hour those lights will be red hot. On this occasion needless to say I dropped the ballet and a couple of other routines before a single paying customer had set foot in the place.

It is also my experience that the places you would expect to feel most comfortable in are often not the safest. You would expect that theatres with reputations to uphold are wonderfully safe. Most are, until you consider the orchestra pit and its twelve-foot drop to a hard concrete floor, or the beautiful backdrop cyclorama behind which is stacked with everything from maintenance scaffolding to the castle from last week's Shakespeare production. One of your friends on stage deciding to hide behind there for some reason could end as a hefty law suit for you and the venue. The venue will naturally blame you for 'telling' them to go behind there and they will probably win. If that happens then I believe that you should lose because you should have been aware of any dangers and ensured that no one would even think about going near them.

By far the easiest way of making things safe is to define your performance area, your stage, in a physical way. I always carry two inch wide white plastic tape. I place this on the stage at a safe limit from drops etc. For instance if you are working a theatre the tape should be placed a minimum of two metres (six feet) from the edge of the stage and at the wings and back. I then constantly deliver the suggestion when the volunteers are doing something that requires them to move around that they will not cross the white line unless specifically told to do so by the hypnotist.

If the stage is accessed from front of house by steps, make sure there is an adequate handrail or that the venue supplies staff to ensure the safety of people using the steps. If the people are not hypnotised then it is the venue, and not you, who are responsible for their safety.

To make sure that you never become victim of a legal action for physical injury; arrive early and spend time checking everything and insist on things being put into good order, never trust anyone to do it for you; it's your neck on the line.

If you use assistants make sure that they are trained well in all aspects of safety.

SHOW TIME!

This part of the book covers the practical side of stage hypnosis. I am presuming that you are going to be performing in a decent sized room or theatre situation, with plenty of room and with a decent sized audience. The reality can be anywhere and any time for any number. The trick of a good performance is to treat everywhere the same, in *your* own reality. My favourite thing is to see every gig as the best theatre show I can imagine: usually a Royal Command Performance at the London Palladium.

Go out and perform to that high standard in a small bar or for a corporate client or club, and you will WOW them.

SETTING THE STAGE

Curtains open, the house lights dim, stage lights come up and your introduction music is played and a voice, (never your own), introduces "... the world's greatest hypnotist!" You walk on stage. This initial impact is very important. The curtains opening on a huge set for a musical production is very dramatic but here's how to use the 'tabs' or curtains in a hypnosis show. Unless absolutely necessary, never have the curtains shut as the house fills. We want to raise emotional expectation in those who have virtually already decided to come up on stage.

As the audience enters the room the first thing they should see is a row of empty chairs waiting for them. The psychological impact of this helps tremendously. There should be nothing else on your stage at this point, no props, no equipment; no you. Just that row of waiting chairs and the expectancy they create. Have the stage lighting low and the shadows deep at this point. In clubs and function rooms you'll even see some people coming over and trying them out unknowingly adding to the expectation and suggestion.

If the curtains have to be shut don't begin your introduction until they are fully open and you have the full effect on your audience.

Your actual introduction should be short and to the point. Musically it can be dramatic but the voice over should announce you simply and quickly: no longer than thirty seconds. For this reason many people use 'Also Spake Zarathustra,' or as it is more commonly recognised, the theme from '2001 A Space Odyssey'. The thing to remember is that as intro-music goes this has definitely been over-used through the years. My music was written specifically for me and the voice over was recorded in a studio by a professional voice over artist, who was a friend and only charged me an arm.

Some performers would consider all this an unnecessary expense for a small venue but the value of this initial impact, in theatre, clubs or even bars and conference rooms, cannot be ignored. Set the scene properly and a quarter of the work in selling yourself is done.

On a purely personal level it is my opinion that scrimping on costs is not the mark of a real professional. If you expect and demand the best fees then you give the best quality and if this cost a few shillings then spend them. Always give value for money.

THE INITIAL PATTER

Your introduction music fades, your audience greets you with a spattering of palm music and you are standing on an empty stage. **Every word you say from now on in is a suggestion**. You are talking not only to their logical, ego-based mind but also (especially in your eventual subjects) their creative mind, the psyche. Everything you say should be clear and concise as well as alluringly magical; sensible and yet nonsensically amazing.

This is without doubt the most important part of your whole show. Get this wrong and you will not have volunteers. No volunteers, no show. There is a supposition that the loneliest job in show business is that of the stand-up comedian, try being a hypnotist with no volunteers. There is nothing you can do, but walk off and hope that there are no journalists out there. I'm not going to give you a script for this because if we all said the same things in the same place, audience confusion over our individuality would increase out of sight. But I am going to tell you what must be in there, and I do mean must!

Don't bore them! I have seen stage hypnotists giving a lecture for over forty minutes on the subject of hypnosis, hypnotherapy, quantum bananas and the meaning of life. The same performers then wonder why they have difficulty in dragging volunteers on stage and keeping the attention of their audience. The reason is of course that they have bored them to death and most are probably well asleep already or back in the bar.

You are not a lecturer. You are an entertainer. If they want to discover the facts of hypnosis let them buy a book, preferably this one. The truth is that most audiences don't want to know. Especially if you are billed as a comedy hypnotist then they have paid good money to be entertained – hopefully with something funny – they don't want an advertisement for your therapy practice. Now I'm not saying that you should only go out and deliver a line of gags, just don't waste time telling the audience anything they don't need to know. Keep it short, sharp and as light as possible.

Your opening remarks, what's known as 'patter' in the business, are extremely important on several levels.

You have to assume that the majority of your audience is unaware of how a live hypnosis show works. Chances are nowadays that they have seen some hypnosis on TV but if they haven't been to a live show it's doubtful they have seen the selection and induction process, most countries still make the broadcasting of this illegal.

So tell them. Point the chairs out and tell them that in a short time twelve, (or however many chairs you have; I would suggest that twelve is a good maximum to work with), people will be sitting here in the state of mind known as hypnosis. Make it a definite statement of fact. It is going to happen; there is no room for doubt.

Reassure them.

LIES TO CHILDREN

The following is not the absolute truth but consider it as telling lies to children. We don't say for instance "Don't sit too close to the television dear because the flickering and small pixilation of the screen may cause your eyes to over strain and possibly in the future could add to a small amount of myopia." Nope, we scream…"Get away from the TV, your eyes will go square!" So rather than going into detail, tell them the small lies which they will think they know and that many hypnotherapists believe to be true anyway as I explain in my book "B A Hypnotist". Tell them that hypnosis is a natural state of mind, is relaxing, akin to day dreaming and that all hypnosis is self hypnosis. . .

Now tell them the truth that after the show everyone that has joined you on stage will feel wonderful. Also assure them that they will be well looked after and given your respect. All this will help to build trust and reduce the fear factor.

They have to trust you. Your obvious confidence in your abilities and assured manner must be such that it engenders this trust and builds a rapport with the audience. For this reason you have to believe in you.

Be 'THE Hypnotist'.

They will have preconceived ideas of how a hypnotist acts and to a point you must be that hypnotist, knowledgeable and calmly confident. Try to appear educated, as some people believe you had to have gone to university to learn all this wonderful stuff! Let them think that, play to their assumption. Don't make any untrue statements but remember that a lot can be said by just saying nothing at all and smiling. Mixing this with a showman like presentation is one of your hardest jobs. Work at being enigmatic.

Lay the blame for any failure directly on the audience.

Okay so we both know that if you fail it is your fault, but no audience must ever think that. Most performers, myself included, tell their audience that hypnosis is impossible if they are in any way mentally incompetent or drunk. I usually make light of this by saying something along the lines of, 'so it's impossible to hypnotise politicians'. You can use; policemen, your management, your committee, the faculty, or any group that best fits the audience you are playing to. This usually gets a laugh and at the same time you have cleverly suggested to them their superiority over the mentioned group because they can be hypnotised. It also shows that you are on their side, building their trust even more. Also it means that should you fail, which you will not, then it is they that do not have the required intelligence, imagination or sobriety to become hypnotised and you can get out of difficult situations by telling them so…and then running very fast.

Make absolutely certain they understand that hypnosis needs co-operation to work.

Tell them they cannot be hypnotised without their ability to let you take them there. Tell them it is not possible to hypnotise them against their will, or make them do anything that goes against their morals or beliefs. I always add that, obviously we are going to get them to experience one or two rather ridiculous and simply silly things and they should have a sense of humour about what they may be asked to do on stage.

In Britain it is a legal requirement to state that all volunteers should be over the age of eighteen and not receiving treatment from their Doctor. Typically the British government has turned pure common sense into a law. Make absolutely sure that they understand that you don't want them to volunteer if they are taking prescribed drugs or suffer epilepsy. Not that hypnosis would alter the effects of most drugs in any way at all, and it definitely could not cause a fit in an epileptic. However if they are up there and have one, try explaining that to their nearest and dearest. If you do this right it actually works in your favour. It makes you look caring and concerned for their safety, increasing once more the trust factor and its accompanying confidence.

Anything else you add to your initial patter is window dressing. This is where your personality shines through; drop in the odd one liner. Targeting yourself is a very good way of doing this, such as saying, "Being a hypnotist is a pain. Every time I comb my hair in a mirror I fall asleep." Not original but it gives you an idea of what I mean. Remember that selling yourself and getting the correct amount of co-operation is the only reason you are doing all this. It may seem that the only way to tell them anything is to lecture. It's not. So just tell them, talking in a relaxed and friendly way. The most important section of your audience will absorb every word out of your mouth right from the very start, those who have already decided to have a go at being hypnotised. They are going to make most, if not all, of your volunteers.

One of my students once commented that if they had already decided to come up with you, why bother to go through all of this and not just walk out, say good evening and ask for volunteers. Great, try it. You may well get lots of volunteers but you could be missing your best performers because they are undecided. Your initial patter will, in most cases, tip the balance with these people. It may even get you a few who hadn't consciously thought that they would volunteer. We are, after all, dealing with a fairly unpredictable animal; an audience.

Keep all this short and succinct. Personally I would not drag this out for more than ten minutes but aim for three or four, that's an awful long time on stage. Be flexible with it, to the point that if you find yourself in the happy position that you don't need all of it you can drop and restructure as you go. Knowing when and where you can do this comes with experience. Getting a feel for your audience has to be learnt by doing, and you will not find that in these or any other pages. Don't worry, it doesn't take long and in a very short time you will become very quick thinking.

For instance my record for making my entrance and hypnotising my first subject is twenty seconds!

Write down your opening patter. Learn it. Be able to present this patter anywhere, anytime, to anyone no matter what without stumbling or stammering.

If you fluff your lines, don't falter, carry on. This is the bridge between them and you and I cannot stress the fact that you will fail or succeed on the strength of their initial impression of you. Of course you have a lot going for you. You are 'THE Hypnotist' and you don't have to *convince* them of this as much as *reassure* them of it. However they do have to like you. They have to trust you and believe in you. Appear confident that you know your stuff; even if you forget everything you wanted to say and are talking complete and utter rubbish. Make it sound authoritative rubbish. They must believe you are the expert or they will not come on stage.

I should just explain the twenty seconds. I was performing at a Junior Ranks Mess in an army base just outside Leicester. Standing at a urinal just before going on I got into a conversation with the corporal standing next me, as one does in that situation. I had quite long hair at the time and was wearing a spangled waistcoat. He somehow guessed correctly that I was the hypnotist and asked me if I'd 'get' a guy called Jim. Apparently this one squadie had never seen a hypnosis show as he had been up on stage every time they had a hypnotist in the mess. Jim had been going around all week telling everyone he was definitely going to see one this time.

He was wrong.

I had the corporal point the poor lad out and, after my introduction had played, went straight up to him. I asked if his name was Jim and when he said it was I almost shouted, "Sleep" at him. Fifty seven seconds including my introduction, and my first subject was spark out over a table. It would have been quicker if I didn't have this limp. Certainly the best proof of your abilities is to do it. I then simply asked who else wanted to be hypnotised and had about twenty people up in seconds.

It is very important here to state that this one particular evening, out of the thousands, was the only time I did not use part or all of my introduction patter.

VOLUNTEER SELECTION

Okay so you are on stage. Intro patter is done and now you need some people up there with you or get the juggling balls out.

There are empty chairs behind you and rows of expectant faces in front of you. I wish, as every stage hypnotist before me has done, that the people in the audience in the right mood to be hypnotised wore some sort of sign, like a huge pointing finger with the words 'They Will Go' on it. The truth is that I have no idea who these people are. Sure you sometimes get the odd person coming up to you before a show telling you how they can't wait to get up there, unfortunately that's rare and you can't really take a poll as they come in. In theatre you probably can't even see them anyway, and if you could and specifically asked them to join you, everyone in the place would suspect a stooge. So how do we 'select' our volunteers from that huge throng?...

TESTS

...You could just ask, and by this time they would come eventually and reluctantly, and your success or failure would be pretty hit and miss. In my experience just asking for volunteers takes forever as they push and cajole each other to go up. It's far simpler to give them a reason to come.

So test them. Give them an example of your power of suggestion and their ability to co-operate.

The main 'test' used by the majority of stage hypnotists is the hand-lock, this, besides being a test is so much more...

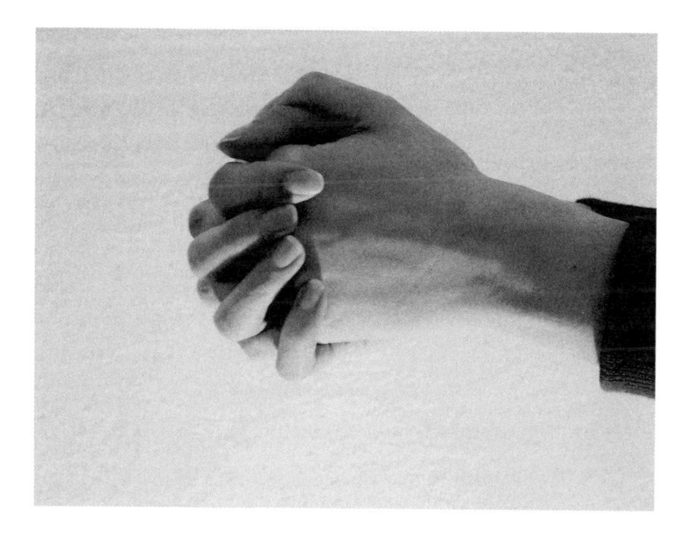

THE HAND LOCK

By far the most common 'test' is the hand lock. Always use this when you have a big audience. It is undeniably the most common because it is the simplest way of convincing them. It's tried tested and, the reason we all use it…it works!

Basically you will 'stick' their hands together, fingers interlocked using simple suggestion. There is only one way of doing this effectively.

Begin by explaining exactly what you are going to do and what the outcome will be. Most importantly, show them.

While telling them to do the actions, I used to use a girl assistant and they used to do the actions as well. Once you've shown them what is going to happen, reassure them that even though their hands are going to be locked together, you can and will unlock them. You could also tell them that their arms may begin to shake, they will for the very receptive because their muscles will become very taut and the blood flow will decrease substantially. Reassure them and tell them it is quite natural. Once again you are adding the suggestion that the result is inevitable.

Tell them that when you count 'one' they will put both hands out in front, fingers and arms outstretched, elbows rigid, and level with their shoulders.

(At this point some may begin to follow your actions, tell them not to. Have them wait, and I always say something along the lines of:

"How I love an eager audience," or under my breath, but loud enough to be heard, say something like: "It's going to be a good night tonight." These are powerful suggestions. Use them whenever you can.)

Now tell them that when you count to two, you want them to put their hands together, fingers interlocked and hands squeezing together tightly.

(Safety first here: I always add that anyone wearing rings should ensure that nothing is digging into them. When you lock their hands you'd be surprised what long nails or engagement rings can do damage wise.)

Finally tell them that on the count of three they will close their eyes and concentrate on the sound of your voice.

(The reason for doing all this is quite simple. Having their arms rigid, hands tight, you are decreasing the blood flow to the fingers and raising the lactic acid. When you finally tell them that they cannot open their hands, they will not only have that powerful suggestion working on their already receptive minds but it will be, for a few moments, mechanically difficult as well.)

Forget anything you have read or been told about dropping your voice an octave or two or talking in a monotonous fashion to deliver suggestion. Totally unnecessary and sounds bloody awful. Clarity and command are far more important. They cannot be allowed to misunderstand or believe that you cannot 'make' them do this. I have included a script for this as with the closing and waking procedures it is important that you, and they, get this right, to get it to work.

Once you have explained everything, do it. Goes like this.

You:

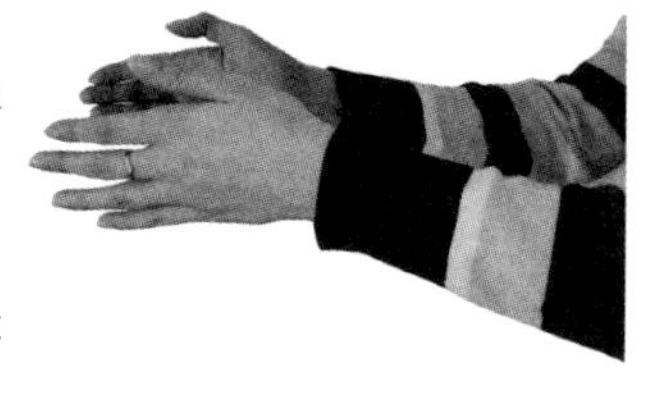

"One: put both hands straight out in front of you."

(Some won't. Ignore them, you won't get them anyway.)

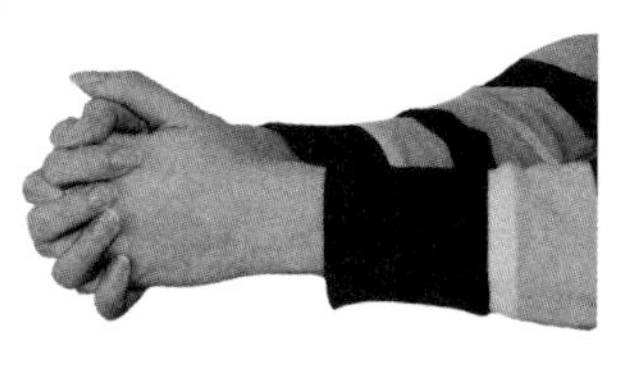

"Two: and lock your fingers together squeezing your fingers tightly together."

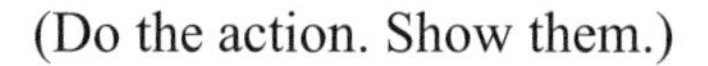

(Do the action. Show them.)

"And..."

"Three: close your eyes and listen to the sound of my voice."

I'd just add here that at this point, without any further words from you, many of the ones whose hands will lock could now be locked by the simple suggestion that they can't open them. In fact if your audience is big enough, say a couple of thousand, then go for it. Tell them that try as hard as they might, they will be totally unable to separate their hands until you tell them they can but you have to judge this well. If you have two thousand people doing it then you may well get twenty to thirty who will not be able to separate their hands. Unfortunately most of your audiences will not be this big, so....

Now begin counting and suggesting that their hands are locking.

You:

“Four: and your hands are locking together tighter and tighter. Five: locking together, super-glued together; locking together tighter and tighter. Six: locking together tighter and tighter.”

Repeating a suggestion in this way is called compounding. Don’t worry, as the opening is the only time you’ll need to do this. It’s the way we naturally learn and it works, ask any good advertising executive. The more the suggestion is repeated the stronger it becomes. Always try and vary it slightly between numbers as this helps to confuse their logical mind, but their creative mind will happily take everything on board. I use a count of twenty, as do others. Any longer and their arms may become so tired that they simply can’t do it any more and you would begin to lose the interest of the rest of the audience.

Don’t count all the numbers. Begin missing out about every third or fourth number. Jump from seven to nine – fifteen to seventeen. There is a very sound reason for this. Not only are you compounding the suggestion for the benefit of their creative mind, but are also aiming to get their logical side to go into virtual shut down. Missing the odd number creates a confused chain of thought that goes something like this.

("Did he say six? I didn't hear him say six. He's an educated person he must have said six. But I didn't hear him say six. Okay so I must be getting hypnotised.")

This obviously happens a lot more quickly but is basically what's going on.

At around the halfway mark of your count tell them to raise their hands above their heads. Right up in the air, stretching to the

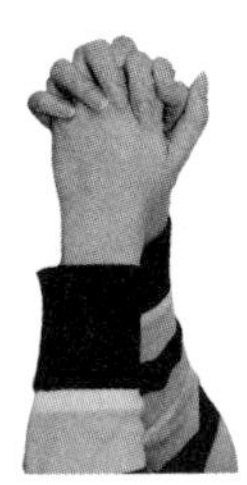

ceiling. Then carry on with your counting and locking. Begin to shorten the gaps between the numbers here and miss sometimes one, sometimes two.

At the end of your count – I go to twenty, and if the venue makes it possible, have them stand. Tell them to stand up and keep repeating the suggestions of tighter and tighter: compound. Then tell them, in a very definite statement that try as hard as they might their hands will not come apart. They are locked together and the harder they try to separate them the more impossible it becomes.

This is using what psychologists call the state of reversed effect. A good example of this is when you are trying to give something up, drink, cigarettes, and the more you think about it the more the reverse happens. You drink and smoke much more while thinking about giving up than ever you did before the reversed effect took hold.

Now and only now, tell them to open their eyes and with their hands locked tightly together to come up on stage and join you.

If you are working a large venue where you may have to wait a while for them to get to you, have some music played. Something stirring. A march is good. (I use brass band music.) And all the time you are suggesting that their hands are locked and that you will separate them easily if they join you. I also add that if they don't want to be here when I've separated their hands then they can just leave. You're safe with saying this. If their hands are locked and they come on stage, then the chances of them leaving are small to minute.

Now in smaller venues and with smaller audiences you may have to be persuasive here. Have the lights turned up so that you can see the ones trying to break their hands apart over their knees or really struggling to pull them. One or two will hide them so you can't see they are locked; it's up to you how you persuade these people to come up. Target these people and tell them not to bother in case they hurt themselves. Repeat that you can and will separate their hands and if they want to return to their seat, then fine. Be friendly and charming and they'll come.

At the end of all this, which in total should take around two to four minutes, five at most, you will have a stage full of people with their hands locked together and their arms in some cases shaking so violently up and down you'd think they were running on alkaline batteries. It's a wonderful sight. It means you are going to get paid and the audience will already be laughing at the expressions on their faces.

I will say however that for this to work properly it's vital that the emotional expectation of your audience has been built up. The times when the hand lock may not work this early is when:

They didn't know you were coming, (you are the surprise!)

There has been little or no advertising done. (Always check that your venue is on the ball. If it is a corporate night or private party, make sure that they have peppered the workplace with your publicity or arrive early and spoil the surprise by telling everyone who will listen who you are and what you do.)

Your publicity pays more attention to who you are rather than what you do. (Remember you are 'THE Hypnotist' first.)

If you don't feel the hand lock will work immediately then use one or both of the following tests but always go back to the hand lock when you can. Why? Because in actuality you have done so much more than just 'test' them.

MORE TESTS

If you find yourself in the unhappy position where the hand lock may not work instantly, you will have to do some preparation work. This can be a little lengthy but add the odd gag and one liner and you'll get through just fine. These next two 'tests' can save the day in a difficult situation.

INDEX FINGER TEST

Nice simple one this. Get them to hold their hands in front of them with their fingers interlocked and elbows bent. Now tell them to extend their index fingers towards the ceiling and to separate the

ends so that they are about an inch apart. Show them what to do. Tell them that in a moment you will count one, two, three, and at the count of three they will squeeze all the fingers together except for their index fingers. Then tell them that what will happen is that their index fingers will come together and touch all of their own accord. Once again demonstrate this and slowly move your index fingers together.

This is a brilliant little test: first because you can easily add some comedy. Pick a guy and ask him if he's a fisherman, if he says no, say, "well you should be if you think that's an inch!" If he says yes, say, "knew it. Well you can stop bragging and move them closer." Ok so it's banal but audiences like it, trust me. And it doesn't take much imagination to improve the gags or add a little innuendo, but like I said. Develop your own style; this is a skeleton, not a script.

The best thing about the index finger test is that it does not rely on anything apart from mechanics. Try it. When you squeeze your other fingers the tendons in your index fingers will tighten and they will come together.

This will definitely weed out the ones who are just not interested because they are the only ones that this won't work for.

Also if you feel that there is a responsive atmosphere in the room you can go straight into a full hand-lock here with no need to tell them what you are going to do. Be careful though and make sure that they are on your side or it will not work and you end up looking quite foolish.

LIGHT AND HEAVY HANDS

If you haven't gone into a full hand-lock from the index finger test explain that the last test shows that they can concentrate; now you are going to test their imaginations. Have them put both hands out; arms straight at shoulder height.

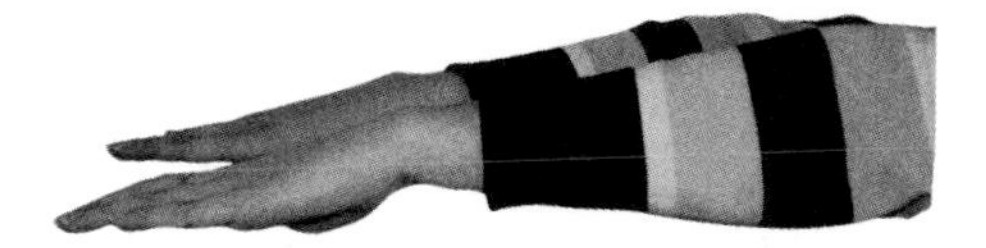

Tell them to turn the right hand palm up to the ceiling and make a tight fist at the end of the arm. Once again safety first, warn women especially not to dig their fingernails into their palms. Tell them to make the arm stiff ensuring that there is nothing underneath such as glasses or bottles.

Now, with the palm facing the floor get them to slightly relax the left arm, keeping it straight but relaxed. At this point ask that those not taking part in the experiment be as quiet as possible to allow the ones taking part to concentrate. This is a double-edged sword. It tells the participants that in your eyes they are important, and also allows you to build a comfortable level of audience control.

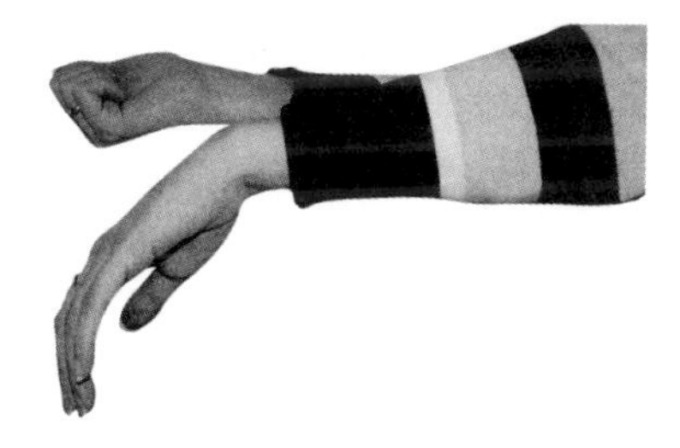

Now tell them to close their eyes and listen to the sound of your voice.

Goes like this:

"I want you to imagine you are holding a heavy steel ball in your right hand. It's getting heavier and heavier and it's being pulled down towards the floor. Your left arm feels like a lighter than air balloon and it's floating up towards the ceiling, becoming lighter and lighter."

Repeat and compound this for a minute or two alternating between arms, between heavy and light. I've seen people suggest that the balloon is tied to the arm, or that they are holding a heavy book, or a bag of sugar. Build on the suggestion, especially the heavy arm, as this will undoubtedly drop as it gets tired. Tell them it weighs the same as two bags of sugar, three; one pound…seven pounds.

Now watch them paying particular attention to the left arm. It should be obvious that we are once again using a mix of suggestion and mechanics. The tense arm will be suffering a reduced blood flow and in the majority of cases will begin to drop after around thirty seconds or so, as the lactic acid builds. Just hold your own arm out tight and make a fist and see how long it is before it begins to drop.

However, the relaxed arm has no real reason to rise. For the majority it won't but watch for the ones where it ends up above their heads. In this test *they* are absolute certainties. Not only have they co-operated but also they are using their imaginations and accepting suggestion.

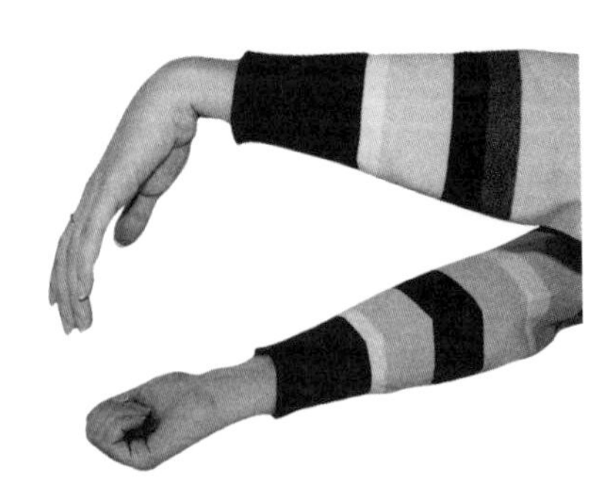

After a minute or two tell them not to move their arms but to open their eyes and look at the difference between the levels of their arms. Now remember you are watching but they are not, make sure you do this when you have some really good potentials out there.

Now tell them if they have a huge or even quite big difference between their arms, they can be hypnotised. That is the moment your marching music begins and you ask them to join you on stage. You will have to be slightly more persuasive here because, unlike the hand-lock, they don't have any pressing need, (like being able to hold a glass), to come up.

In most cases I would, once they are up, do a hand-lock. If you only have a few, sit them down and do it. If there are lots, do it standing up! It is still the easiest way of whittling down the fakers and d-heads.

FINAL SELECTION

By now we should have a stage full of hand-locked subjects, say thirty. Now we want to whittle them down to a manageable level, twelve is a good maximum although don't worry if you have less than this.

Get them to drop their hands in front of their chests with their elbows bent and keep telling them that their hands are locking together tighter and tighter. Now be observant and pick your final subjects carefully as the whole show depends on them. There are obvious 'types' that you really don't need; the things to look for are the effects of:

Drink, Drugs and Fear.

Drunks can pass out or vomit. Drug takers can pass out or vomit. Terrified people can pass out, vomit, burst into tears and spontaneously lose control of their bladder or bowels. If you are not sure get rid of them!

Here are a few obvious things to look for: smell of alcohol, if you can smell it chances are they have had enough or perhaps too much. One thing is for sure, you shouldn't have had any, so the smell should be noticeable: distended pupils and unexpected shaking. You can expect the arms to be shaking, you've even suggested they will, but if they appear to be shaking all over this could be caused by fear or by certain drugs. Distended or enlarged pupils especially under bright stage lighting could point to drugs or other physical conditions that you don't want to have to deal with on stage.

The volunteers I'd go for are those who have a look of happy bafflement about them. They are usually smiling and are looking at their hands and you in a bemused way. Once you've seen this 'look' up close, you will instantly recognise it. Trust your instincts.

So now you need to find the best subjects. That is those who will readily accept your suggestions and as far as possible make your stage and your show look good. The test for suggestibility is simple. Walk up to a likely subject, being as friendly as possible, smile and say hello nicely, grab their locked hands and while always suggesting they are locking tighter and tighter, try and push your middle finger between their palms. If it goes right through and past them with little or no resistance, you've got a faker or someone not really 'into' it. Simply shake their hands apart and tell them you're sorry but they are not in the right mood and would they please return to their seat. Notice, I say tell them. Don't ask in this situation, you have to have complete control of the stage; *it* belongs to *you*. For this reason I would always do this over the microphone so that the audience knows they are not suitable. They won't dare stay to cause you trouble as they would then look foolish, not you.

If there doesn't appear to be any effects of the three things I mentioned earlier, and it's virtually impossible to push your finger between their palms, you can use them. If, however, you can't easily try their hands with your finger, look for pure white knuckles and the forearm 'shakes'. They will be easy to work with and will accept suggestions readily and easily. Simply separate the hands of everyone else and tell them they can go back to their seats and enjoy the show.

INDUCTIONS

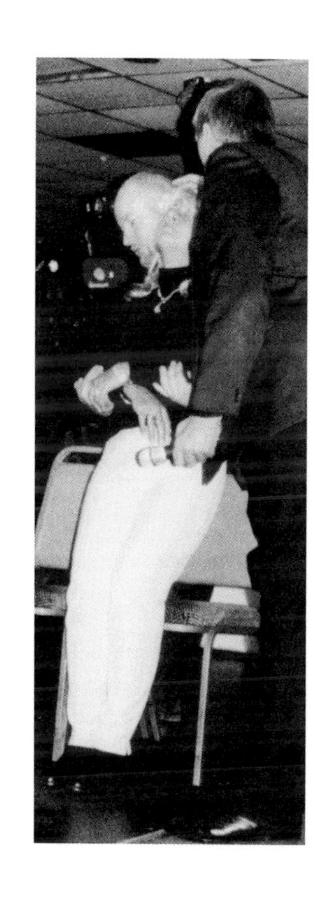

≈

Now we reach the point where we will appear to lead our volunteers into the state of hypnosis. And because we have to do this carefully and slowly, as so many hypnosis books tell us to do, there will now be a lull in proceedings while you do this. I just wish you could see me grinning. Something should be obvious to you by now but in case you have missed it, I will make it clear.

Stage Hypnosis requires that your friends on stage are using their creative abilities and have, for the moment, put aside any limiting factor supplied by their conscious brain allowing them to accept your suggestions.

You have not stapled their hands together. They are not tied or handcuffed. There is absolutely no reason for them not to be able to loosen and separate their hands. Apart from the fact that they truly believe they can't.

See it yet?

That's right. If you have locked their hands together using suggestion and nothing else, then they are already in the mental state you need them to be in.

They are already hypnotised!

Hypnosis, we must remember, is a state of mind. Although your audience expects to see people in a state reminiscent of sleep, and your friends on stage expect the same. It is not necessary. Relaxation has become a part of hypnosis because it is the usual symptom of the state in the therapy room (always suggested by the hypnotist). All very well for what a friend of mine calls 'relaxotherapy'. Hypnosis does not need it. But that is what your audience has paid for, and that is what they are going to get. You as 'THE Hypnotist' must know that it isn't the cause, merely a reaction to your suggestion. Once they have accepted a suggestion to this degree then they will accept ninety nine percent of all your suggestions.

Induce means to cajole, persuade, to lead. You, my friend, have already done that. Especially if you have a full blown hand-lock! Okay so your audience does not want to see you simply going up to people snapping your fingers and saying sleep! Oh it would work without doubt and in the right circumstances, with the right crowd, you can do just that. Try it; although you've been working for ages the audience will believe they witnessed that ideal of all hypnotists INSTANT INDUCTION!

You can add the finger snapping if you want and, if they are standing, they will instantly become relaxed and probably fall on you, or if you are incredibly unlucky fall off the stage into the orchestra pit or someone's lap. But besides being dangerous it isn't what the majority of audiences want. They want at this point to see something dramatic, something astounding, above all they want theatre, and you being an exemplary showman / woman will give them just that. Only you will know that hypnosis as such has already been 'induced' and that what you are actually doing now is 'deepening' the state, and making yourself look good.

I should say however that intensifying their state would be more accurate. The deepening is more than a little deceptive even though it's generally accepted in the field. In fact they are going nowhere and you can just as easily say go higher and higher, or wider and wider, or more sideways. What we are actually doing is intensifying the mood: making their reality more vibrant.

It's a misnomer using the term 'instant induction' at all. All inductions are of course instant, as all thoughts are instant, or in some cases faster. There is a definite and definitive point of change. I can't describe it here, and doubt it would show even on video but it does happen and when you hypnotise you will see, feel, sense it, or maybe little fairies will whisper to you, I don't know, but I promise it will happen.

The following induction's all work splendidly well on stage. I often use a combination of them as this adds light and shade even to this part of your show.

THE DROP BACK

I have seen a few variations of this in print and on stage. In the old days it was often referred to as the sway test and the way they did it was damn boring and slow. Today's audiences do not want to see you repeating ad nauseam that the volunteer is beginning to sway towards you, or away. Gently swaying volunteers is boring. They want action and drama.

Stand your volunteers in a line shoulder to shoulder facing the audience. If you have any with violently shaking hands repeat the tighter and tighter suggestion every now and then and see if you can get them looking as if their arms will drop off. The more they shake the more your audience will laugh. Don't over milk this but just drop it in as you are organising things.

Once you have the line complete, get them to stand with their knees and heels together and tell them to pick a point above eye level and to stare at it. In theatres and larger clubs this is easy. Tell them to look directly at one of the lights. Even in a smaller venue use a light for preference. All this is doubly important if you haven't used a hand-lock and are relying on your capabilities of inducing hypnosis without it.

Now tell them, over the microphone, that you are going to hypnotise them. Tell them that their eyes are getting heavy and wanting to close but they will not close until you tell them to. Tell them that no matter what happens they will not take their eyes away from the light. The light is important because we want the main thing on their minds to be shutting out that bloody light by closing their eyes. Staring stings after a while and the majority of people will have tears rolling down their cheeks in seconds. You are also in a perfect situation to check whether they are paying attention and following your instructions or just up for a giggle, watch for the ones who are blinking and or looking everywhere except for the light. Remove them now.

While doing this you are telling them that you will go to each in turn and close their eyes.

Tell them that you will count three, two, one, and that on the count of one, they will fall gently back into your arms instantly falling into a state of deep relaxation, of deep sleep. Make these lines a statement, a command not a plea. Phrase it as if it has already happened. Raise their expectation. Make sure you reassure them that they will not fall and that you will catch them. You can do this on or off mic., talking quietly to them when you are standing next to them.

I should mention here that having a Neuro-muscular condition I have never caught the subjects myself. I always had an assistant to do it, or on the odd occasion used volunteers from the audience who were not being hypnotised. If you do this for whatever reason make sure they know exactly what is expected of them.

Look for your first 'victim'. There will be one, there always is, who is either swaying already or whose eyes are beginning to shut.

Go and stand close to them. Tip their head back and tell them to

close their eyes. The best will just go but after them you'll have to help things along a little.

Tap their back gently and rhythmically at about the rate of a heartbeat, this helps to confuse their already perplexed conscious.

Tell them to see the stars, which is precisely what they are seeing after staring into the light. This compounds their faith in you as being brilliant and psychic. Now count down from three. Do this quickly. Then tell them they are going backwards like this.

You:

"One, two, three going back, back, back..." Now if you have to (it will be rare that you do) pull them back, hand on shoulder. They will instantly begin to drop backwards.

Good subject's knees will stay fairly straight and they go back almost board like, showing you absolute trust. If their knees begin to buckle this doesn't mean you've blown it somewhere. Don't worry. Put your foot behind their heels and pull a little harder and they will come back anyway. In both cases the moment they over-balance say, "Sleep!"

With the conscious so confused it is no longer working with absolute focus, their creative mind will grab hold of any suggestion that promises respite from the confusion.

If possible always drop at least one person back in this way. It will help to convince all the others that what you are about to do to them will work. Often the more you do drop back the faster it happens, as the expectation, and knowing the others are 'going', is a great convincer.

When they are on their back, gently separate their hands and say soothingly, "That's right, just sleep." Then move onto your next 'victim'.

Of all induction's this is the most dramatic and visual.

CHAIR DROP BACK

In those situations where you don't have room to lay twelve people down on stage just 'drop' them into their chairs in a sitting position.

Stand them as before but now with the back of their knees against

the seat of the chair. Tell them that when you reach the number one they will drop into a comfortable sitting position in the chair behind them.

Either you or an assistant should now stand behind the chair to prevent it tipping. As before tilt their head back and count.

When you get to the number one grab their elbows and gently but firmly pull them against the chair. The seat against the backs of their knees will force the knees to bend and as they drop into the chairs you can pull back on their elbows and with your chest, tip their head forward.

This looks almost as dramatic as a full drop-back but is far safer and easier to perform in confined spaces.

A small visual gag can be added here by resting the head of one person on the shoulder of the person next to them.

HANDSHAKE

A guy running a hypnotherapy course first demonstrated the hand-shake induction to me some twenty years ago. It was the only time I saw him fail. It has to be said that he did this three days into the course by which time everyone had been hypnotised by everyone else around fifty times and the emotional expectation was at a level most hypnotists would kill their grandmothers for. However, with a little practice it looks so good it is virtually unbelievable. You just have to get the timing right.

Grab the hand of your volunteer and ask them if they have ever seen anyone hypnotised with a handshake. (I have been told it is possible to do this without saying a word; however I have never seen it done without saying this, or something like it first. So prove me wrong.)

Take their hand and shake it three times fairly vigorously.

On the third shake pull them towards you and give the command, "Sleep". The theory is that this action confuses the conscious mind

to such an extent that it 'cuts out' for an instant and the much more suggestible creative mind comes to the fore.

If they accept the suggestion they fall against you, so be prepared to ease them down and make sure you are firmly balanced and have somewhere to put them afterwards.

I know of at least three hypnotists who are given credit for this particular induction, but am inclined to think that this was possibly one of the first, if not *the* first, of all the dramatic approaches.

NOTE: This is NOT the Erickson handshake which is a much gentler and less dramatic affair as I demonstrate on my masterclass.

HAND-SNAP

This is for those occasions where you have no room to stand behind the chairs or to lay the volunteers down and you have performed a hand-lock with them sitting down.

Have them hold their locked hands out in front of them.

Stand in front of the volunteer and hold your left hand around three inches above theirs.

Point your right index finger towards your left at their eye level and tell them to watch that finger. Raise the right-hand slowly, repeating, "Watch my finger, watch my finger."

Now timing is everything. They will follow your finger at first with their eyes only. Just as they begin to tip their head back to be able to see your finger, snap the fingers of your left hand and drop it on top of theirs.

At the same time with your right hand pull their head forward and give the command, "Sleep!"

If you are holding the microphone in your right hand please be careful not to hit them with it. Okay so it would certainly put them into a state of unconsciousness but you will have to explain the dent after the show.

MAGNETIC HANDS

I use this when, for whatever reason I can't use a hand-lock, or have been the surprise guest at a party. It's my preferred induction with groups when I'm coaching and even in class with students. It is by far the slowest induction here but it does work wonderfully well.

Have them sit. Tell them to put their hands out in front with their elbows bent and their fingers together outstretched. Make sure they

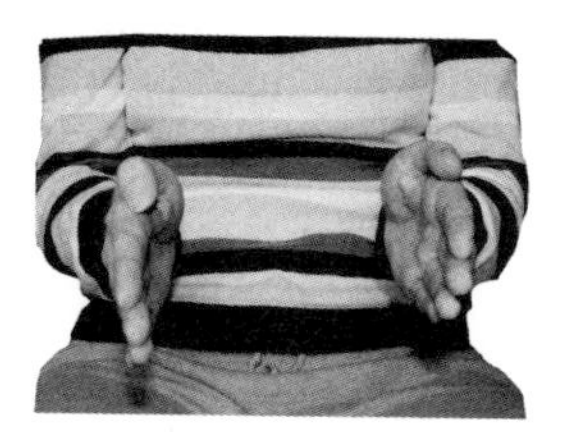

don't rest their arms or elbows on their lap as they need free movement.

Tell them to close their eyes; this helps their concentration and stops visual distraction. Now begin to suggest that their hands are being pulled together by those magnets, getting closer and closer; being irresistibly drawn together and, at the moment, the very instant they touch, they will feel a huge wave of relaxation spread through every nerve muscle and fibre. Tell them that when this

happens their hands will fall gently into their laps and their heavy heads will drop forward as they enter a wonderfully relaxing state of sleep.

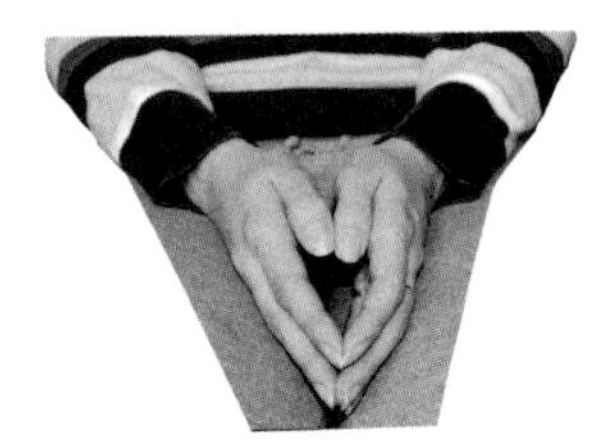

This can take a long time with some people; however you can quicken the process a little.

Watch them carefully and, providing you have some movement of the hands towards each other, wait until the hands are an inch or two apart and then gently pull them together with your free hand. Push them firmly down into their laps at the same time in a soft but commanding voice, say, "That's right. Just sleep and let go."

The success rate with this method is about the same as with the other inductions, in fact more so when not actually 'performing on stage'. It's only down side being that it is less dramatic and slower.

You may also have to rely more than usual on your 'deepening' technique to actually tip them over into the hypnotic state, but don't worry, you would only use this in situations where the audience is smaller and therefore much more intimate.

Happily with a smaller audience you should have complete control and can usually get away with murder.

'SLEEPING' AND STANDING

During the course of your show you will undoubtedly have occasion to have them 'sleeping' while they are standing up. Many hypnotists, me included, make the first time they do this, an 'event'.

I will ask my best subject if they believe they can go to sleep standing up. Ignore the answer, it doesn't matter. I then put my hand on their shoulder and lightly hold their clothing. I then give the sleep command, quickly followed by saying, "You can stand, just balance yourself the way you do when you are fully awake. You will not fall over."

You can get a lot of audience reaction from this. Often the other volunteers will be looking rather pensively at this guy or girl standing next to them, rock still, with their eyes shut. Now ask the next person if they think it can happen to them, snap them under and say to the audience. "Oh look. It did!" This way you are in full control of the safety of your volunteers and can still be entertaining.

As the show goes on you will simply be able to say, "Sleep and stand where you are." This gets wonderful audience reaction when you are working a venue such as a bar or restaurant where you can send them out into the audience. It's one thing watching people being hypnotised on the stage a distance away, and quite another when they are right next to you.

DEEPENING THE STATE

While checking for the previously mentioned ways to recognise hypnosis, you should 'deepen,' or more accurately, intensify the state they are now in. This is how I do it, you can work your own method but I know this works, because it has a few thousand times. Only experience can tell you how far to take this. When I first started in the game and wasn't so confident in my abilities, I would sometimes drag this out to the point that some of the volunteers went to sleep and ended up snoring. Have confidence that this can be done quite quickly with the desired effect.

The following suggested patter can even induce the people you didn't quite catch.

"I'm going to begin counting, and with every number I go past, with every deep breath you take, with every firm beat of your heart, you are doubling the relaxation you are feeling now. There is only the sound of my voice and nothing bothers or disturbs you apart from the sound of my voice. Ten, deeper and deeper, nine, with every deep breath, eight, with every firm beat, seven with every number going deeper and deeper: more and more relaxed; five," (the missed number again) and so on to one.

Always, always count down to put them in; up to bring them out. There is no reason for this other than when I haven't done it this way I've seen the odd confused attitude.

While all this is going on I have music played. I like modern music and have had my tracks exclusively composed and recorded for me, however anything will do. The volunteers don't need it, you don't need it. It is simply there to fill the odd space when you take a breather; helps to add atmosphere and will usually keep your audience quiet. I've seen just about everything used from Gregorian chant to the time when a tape broke and my roadie used

'Another One Bites the Dust'. The Queen track worked wonderfully well but in general go for something more laid back, anything else might well distract your subjects and make the deepening harder for you.

Just a mention here of subliminal messages in the music. For a start, if you can find a recording studio ruthless and well enough equipped to do them, they'll cost you a fortune and the studio is ripping you off. They don't work. The famous coke bottle on a single frame of film was a hoax, an advertising scam, and several governments have tried everything from teaching language to increasing psychic capabilities with them, they do not work. Okay you can put a second voice on the recording and duet with it as I've seen done, but this is nothing more than window dressing. A good hypnotist hypnotises. They don't need anything else.

Hypnosis and subliminal programming have nothing at all in common. Hypnosis works.

Back to your deepening. There are some great opportunities here for a little comedy especially if you used the drop-back: Crossing a guy's legs by lifting his trouser bottoms or lifting an arm and getting people to 'hug' each other. The odd suggestion that they are next to their sweetheart can be funny, especially when, for some reason, two members of the same sex cuddle up close. Use your imagination but don't go further than your audience will stand for. And be careful when you are waking them up, homophobia is real and you don't want a violent reaction.

On the count of number one stop the music and deliver your first proper suggestions. Take my advice and use these in this order.

"If for any reason you have to leave the building in a hurry or an emergency, or if you just leave to go home normally, the moment you step outside you will return completely and absolutely back to the state you were in before you came up on stage." (Repeat this; it shows you care for them and covers your back in case there is a fire, or the revolution starts.) A good tip here is to video this. Now if they are hypnotised they will accept this suggestion. If they then leave and try to claim that your 'spell' made them run naked down the street throwing marshmallow at people then it can be argued that this could not have been your fault as 1) They were outside the building and would have reacted to the suggestion and behaved as they normally would, 2) If they did not take that suggestion then they were not hypnotised and could not have been influenced by any other suggestion. (You know when this book was originally written that wouldn't have been necessary. Sad, isn't it?)

To avoid confusion, tell them that you will touch them on the shoulder when you are talking to them.

Tell them that from now on, until they leave the stage, when you say sleep, they will instantly return to this state, going even deeper than the time before. And that when you say, one, two wide-awake they will be wide-awake and perfectly able to move normally in every way with their eyes wide open.

(Safety tip) Never allow anyone to move around with their eyes closed. I once witnessed a hypnotist doing a ballet routine and noticed three of his volunteers dancing with their eyes shut! I noticed, but he didn't! Luckily he got away with it but being as he had the press in the house I could see the reputation of 'THE Hypnotist' taking a very big fall and spent a very uncomfortable two minutes. Always remember, safety first.

From now on you can use a snap of your fingers, a klaxon horn or the sound of Big Ben instead of the word sleep. Saying sleep is easier and it's expected so tell them now what will happen when they are told to sleep, or when you click your fingers.

I sometimes stand in front of them with my hand out and just lower it. They 'go'. Or try standing with your back to the audience and just mouth the word 'sleep'. It never ceases to amaze me how attentive the psyche can be when it's allowed to take charge. Try anything and everything; they will all work. In fact the biggest rule in this whole book is that *there are NO rules* and that what works, works.

DELIVERING SUGGESTIONS

It should be obvious that if they accept the super suggestion then every book that tells you that you have to bore your audience to death by repeating and compounding suggestions is so much rubbish. However, there are still some points you must know on how suggestion works.

“Use your fork!”

A suggestion made to the two-year-old, which is repeated until eventually; by around the age of thirty, they do use their fork...mostly.

The suggestion is repeated and every time it is, it compounds, to eventually become a compulsion, a virtually instinctive action. The suggestion has been accepted. Hypnotherapists will sometimes use this repeated form of suggestion, compounding one on top of another until the desired effect is achieved. This is an often slow, cumbersome and laborious process but can make lasting positive changes if carried on long enough.

However, we can also accept suggestions, even if only hearing them once. Take the case of a young child who is in a very emotional state after a fall and runs to a parent for comfort and support. The adult is busy on the phone and yells at the child to be quiet. The suggestion easily finds it way into the child’s exposed psyche and, because our psyche is so smart – it’s really, really stupid – the child's mind devises a way to accept the suggestion. It could happen that the child then develops a terrible stammer, or just stops talking altogether. Stammering is an excellent excuse for keeping quiet and accepting and acting on a very powerful suggestion. This may seem impossible but I have personal knowledge of just such a case.

On Stage we don't have the time to compound too much if we want the show to flow and move well. You are only on stage for a limited time and don't want to lose the attention of your audience, so speed is of paramount importance. Unless of course you have an inexhaustible supply of gags and one-liners you can drop in here and there to keep the whole thing going. If this is the case, be a comic. It's a lot less hassle and ultimately you'll stand a better chance of landing your own TV show. So, don't compound.

Vocal tone is important but not vital. It will help if you dramatise a little by emphasising the more emotive words but you don't have to talk in monotones, sing songs or use the 'hypnotic voice' – that one always makes me chuckle. Clarity and a little command is all that is really needed. This is easy to achieve as you have the advantage of having your voice amplified through a microphone and speakers. Set correctly with a little bass, and absolutely no reverb or echo, the sheer volume can give your vocal tone the required feeling of command and authority it will need. Be firm and don't shout. This is the command of a schoolteacher rather than that of a drill sergeant.

The attention span of your subjects should also be taken into account. Remember that they are, once induced into a hypnotic state, wholly concentrated on you. And if they have accepted the super suggestion you will not have to repeat what you say interminably to get an idea across.

As we said earlier, persuasion and authority are vital when delivering your suggestions. Keep things simple and clear. Short phrases are much easier than long diatribes. It's almost as if you were a painter using the subject's imagination as your canvas: a minimalist painter, using as little material and effort as possible.

Say for instance that you want them to imagine being on a beach. Be definite and paint your picture for their imagination, but use as few brush strokes as possible. I would say the following:

"You are on a beach. Feel the hot sun. Go on...stretch out in your deck chair and enjoy that relaxation."

Let's break this down and look at it.

"You are on a beach." Notice that this is delivered as a statement of fact. You are placing them there in their mind's eye.

"Feel the hot sun."

This is another statement using not only their imaginations but also the fact of their physical condition and surroundings. When hypnotised, most people experience a slight rise in body temperature, couple this with the stage lights and they are going to feel warm anyway, use this to compound your suggestion rather than repetition.

"Go on...stretch out in your deck chair and enjoy that relaxation." Stretch your words and suggest the relaxation. Now you are being persuasive, once again using their condition as they are already relaxed and are probably enjoying it anyway. It's amazing but twelve or so people stretching out on chairs on stage will already have begun to raise giggles from your audience. Hopefully one or two of the guys will decide to unbutton their shirts; it's amazing how big a laugh that gets.

Now you can add to your picture. Describe palm trees, sand, sea, whatever. Tell them that they are eating ices; make them alcoholic (it's funnier), or get them to take a cool drink because they are feeling so hot. You are compounding the suggestion, eliciting a response and causing action in one simple scenario.

If you deliver your suggestion in a compelling way then they will comply. Be clear. Unless working your own local area do not use colloquialisms. Be precise. Tell them exactly what is expected of them. Remember you are responsible for what goes in, try and be responsible as far as is possible, for what comes out!

THE SUPER SUGGESTION

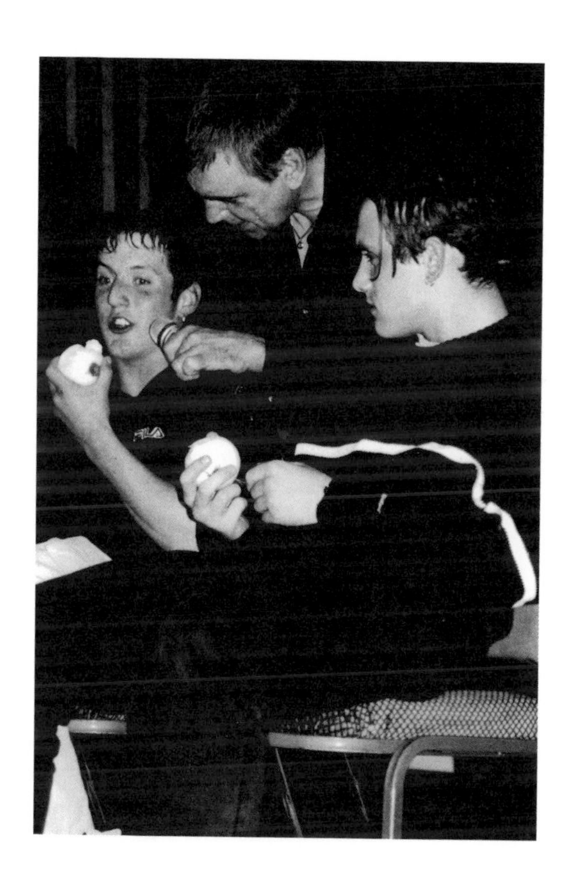

Deliver this one correctly and you can forget about compounding for the rest of your show. Compound (repeat) this suggestion a few times then forget it. And if you are a curiosity reader already in the game, please don't write telling me you invented this. I have a book dated 1867 that almost word for word gives this phrase, so if you wrote that then perhaps you should think of retiring?

It goes like this.

"From this moment **everything** I say to you. **Every single thing** I say, no matter how silly or stupid it seems will **instantly become your reality**. **Everything I say** will **instantly** become your **reality**." (Emphasise the words in bold letters.)

As I said repeat this two or three times. Just a warning here: When they accept this suggestion, which, having locked their hands, dropped them back and deepened them, you can be absolutely sure they will, be very careful what you say to them. Everything you say will now be taken as an irresistible suggestion. If you trip and fall or a spotlight falls on your head, for God's sake don't shout, "Shit!" You may have one hell of a mess to clean up! And saying anything stronger which begins with the letter 'f' just doesn't bear thinking about.

Just joking, but **be careful**.

THE WAKE UP PROCEDURE

So, we've had them up, had them hypnotised, helped them to make complete arseholes of themselves for an hour or two. We have been careful and observant and safe and we've finished our last routine. Now we come to what is – without any doubt whatsoever – THE MOST IMPORTANT PART OF THE WHOLE SHOW…not least because your reputation can be completely destroyed by not tidying up properly. Most importantly though is the fact that if you screw up here it is mine and everyone else's reputation that gets stuffed as well. Done correctly you will ensure that no one will ever be in a position to claim against that huge public liability insurance you have, (in Britain you won't get a licence without it) or sue the pants off you. And THE HYPNOTIST won't get cancelled by the people who can't tell the difference between you and the guy who just says "One two wide awake."

In the past it was a very common ending to leave volunteers still reacting to a post hypnotic suggestion. (That is to suggest that after leaving the stage for a final time, your volunteers will react to a certain piece of music, or a word from you, such as 'Goodnight!') It was just such a post hypnotic that started the Campaign against Stage Hypnosis in Britain, after the unfortunate death of a volunteer later that night. The inquest came to the conclusion that there was no connection between the girl's death from an epileptic fit and the hypnosis, but her family didn't believe it and has now become a thorn in the side of stage hypnotists in the UK. Fortunately they have been very quiet whilst I have been writing this, but they are still there.

Take my advice. Never, ever, leave your volunteers with a post-hypnotic suggestion unless that is the positive one of feeling wonderful and refreshed. Always clean up. (Note: In Britain it will almost always be a part of the legal requirements of your licence. Unless you have a lot of money, a very good lawyer, or absolutely no sense; don't test it.)

I believe that there is simply only one way of doing the 'Wake up' cleanly and effectively, so I'll follow this with the only script as such in this book. There is no reason not to do this exactly word for word as it's written here. There is everything to gain from doing so and a lot to lose from not. This wake up has been formulated mostly by hypnotherapists and is widely used by many schools. There is a very good reason for this – it works. Remember that we are dealing with the belief factor in your volunteers. You don't know them so you don't know what they believe. Say they had a friend who after being on stage with a hypnotist was left with a tremendous headache. They may well believe that this will happen to them. The last thing you need is for people to be complaining of feeling ill after a show so don't let it happen.

The following script will of course slow things up tremendously. Fine, show's over anyway. You can turn this to your favour by telling the audience that the most important thing you have to do is to ensure that your friends on stage are woken properly and are fine. Your reputation and esteem will go through the roof, as will your repeat bookings! Trust me on this. Use the wake up procedure and then individually ask them how they feel. A good skit here is to ask them how long they've been on stage. When they've been there for two hours and they think it's five minutes, your audience will love the confusion on their faces and it brings the whole thing back up, so you lose nothing and presenting yourself as 'mister nice and caring guy', you gain everything. But also I do this for something that is important to me – I actually care. Those people at the very least deserve your respect, they have given you the most important thing they have, their trust and belief, and they should be looked after.

THE WAKE UP SCRIPT

You:

"In a moment I am going to bring you back to full awareness. I will count one to five and on the number five you will open your eyes and stretch, feeling completely refreshed and alive. It's like you've had eight hours sleep. However being hypnotised is not sleep and when you next go to bed you will sleep better than you have for years and awake at the appropriate time feeling refreshed and revitalised. (See note [1]) Everything is returned to normal in every way.

So, one!

Every nerve, every muscle becoming less relaxed.

Two:

Feel that huge surge of energy go right through your body.

Three:

Take a deep, deep breath of cool, clear, mountain air, feeling that energy giving oxygen going through every nerve muscle and fibre.

[1] Okay so this is a post-hypnotic. But it's one that you can get away with because it's for the benefit of their well being. Never say, "When you go to bed tonight." They could be working a graveyard shift. Same with waking up in the morning, use "the appropriate time." There are of course other post-hypnotic suggestions you can use; such as telling them they have a nice taste in their mouth if they have eaten some substance that could do otherwise, or that they won't feel embarrassed by the things their friends tell them they have done. All these are positive in effect and as such would be completely acceptable. If you do nothing else from this book, do this right, please.

Four:

You can feel that cool clear mountain water washing through your head, your chest, your body. Your stomach and chest are clear. Your head is clear. Your throat and nose are clear. Your eyes are bright and shiny and…

Five! WIDE AWAKE!"

Make every word a direct command. Lift your voice as you go through the numbers and emphasise the emotive words and action; words such as 'clear', 'energy' and 'bright and shiny'.

YOUR SHOW

Okay so now your volunteers are 'under' and hopefully your audience has stuck around. Now you can 'wake' them up, individually, and get them on the seats and begin your show proper. The whole thing so far will take anything from ten to fifteen minutes and you've had ample opportunity to add flair, showmanship, theatre and comedy from the instant you first set foot on stage.

Now we can get to work. You have your hypnotised people; you have your stage. By now your audience should be giving you their entire attention. Now, with the help of your new friends, you are going to give them a show.

Start with something simple, something easy. You are working with a part of their mind that the average person hasn't used since childhood, some, not even then. Nurture it and build.

I am going to be careful here not to give you too many scripts, for two reasons:

1) I want you to be as original as possible.

2) My business agent assures me that I can't afford the time in court proving that no routine is really original.

It's better to look at it from a performance point of view.

Your first few routines should have three elements.

Visual

Get them doing something that the audience can see the results of. Riding bikes or horses is a favourite of many performers, getting them to watch an imaginary play or film, either incredibly happy or sad. Getting them to laugh or cry is always visually good and you are using the fact that they are in an entertainment venue to great effect.

Vocal

Get them doing something that you can ask them questions about, or anything that gives them the opportunity to speak. The routines that spring to mind instantly are forgetting a number or their name. Talking in an unusual or imaginary language or believing that they are someone famous addressing the audience. Tell them to be somewhere else and get them to describe it; preferably somewhere they would be unlikely to be familiar with, like the Moon, Mars or the planet Zog.

Funny

Whether billed as a comedy hypnotist or not, you will be expected to get the volunteers to do things that are funny. That is the way it goes. That, and only that, is what your audience has paid for. You are kidding yourself, and doing them a disservice if you believe anything else.

There is a very good reason for having these elements in your first two or three routines: your evaluation of the people on stage: watch everything like a hawk. By the time you have got through your opening routines you should know who is physically good, who is verbally good, and which of your friends have the best wit. After all you have spent hours formulating your routines; planning; practising your asides and gags. If you now pick the wrong person for a specific routine then you've wasted all that time.

Obviously you will, or have seen as many hypnosis shows as possible. So you will undoubtedly 'borrow' one or seventy-three routines. Just some advice on plagiarism: I was once told, in my early days, to 'steal the best, reject the rest'. This is fine to a point.

No one can copyright a basic idea. The essential basis of the routine is the idea and many of the routines we modern acts use originate with people such as the great Robert Halpern, and others like David Casson, Dave Elman was a stage innovator in the States, and Ormond McGill.

But inspiration can come from anywhere and most of us cross over. We hypnotists use very similar routines because there is only so much that you can do with the volunteers' imaginations. But do it your way.

Every magician has a false thumb-tip, but what makes each magician unique is the way they use it and what they say whilst doing their tricks, and the odd bit of stealing often goes unnoticed because of it being wrapped up in originality.

There are far fewer hypnotists than magicians and comics, and while it may be fine to take an idea, if you then present that idea word for word, exactly as you saw it done; same gags, same presentation, then someone is going to find out and you are well on the way to getting bits of your nether regions sued off!

Besides that, this is just bad manners and can cost you other bits of anatomy should you get hit legally. Anyway it shows a distinct lack of talent and you should begin looking for that Yak farm.

So I am not going to give you fully scripted routines but will tell you what you can do in your show.

Some of these ideas will be familiar; some may not. Remember I'm generalising. If you like, I'm giving you a thumb-tip, what you do with it is up to you. From these basics there really are a million and one routines, probably more.

SHOW STRUCTURE

I know your show isn't a musical or play and as such can't be scripted for everything to be done in a specific way at a specific time. Think of it as a mental wrestling match, we know the moves but the dance is ad-libbed to the roar of the crowd.

But it is a stage show and, especially if you are lucky enough to have lighting and sound engineers working with you they have to have at least an idea of what you are going to do. I usually 'script' my shows by writing down the routines I wish to do, in shorthand form:

Intro

Hypnotise

Hot and cold, etc

At the side of this I put any music to be played and next to these put my lighting requirements if needed.

I employ my own roadie / stage manager who, from the wings, takes care of all this for me. Personally I think this is vital for the value and look of the thing and to retain the professionalism. Nothing looks more amateurish than a lone performer arriving and setting up their equipment and using a remote control, or worse not using one.

Just look at the top line performers on stage. Do you see Tom Jones or David Copperfield using a laptop? And what happens when the inevitable goes wrong, and the system crashes or your battery runs out on the radio mic., or one of your volunteers hides behind a speaker and pulls a plug? There is nothing professional about stopping to fix something or just as bad carrying on without. Stage hypnosis has more than its fair share of such low grade performers. Don't be one of them.

The argument against this is being unable to ad-lib. Well that's only the case if you don't have a good roadie or assistant, or if you haven't bothered to rehearse them well. A really good roadie is a boon in situations where you are dealing with several crew. If I decide on the spur of the moment to change things I only have to let one person know and they take care of the others. I have an idiot board for myself with some reminders of the order I've chosen; sometimes I have this in a huge folder on stage entitled, 'THE IDIOT'S GUIDE TO HYPNOSIS'. Pick this up and your audience think it's a gag, they'll never know that you've forgotten what comes next. I am prone to go off on a tangent and one of my roadie's, Jim, made his own idiot card, which said 'You Bastard' for the times when I gave him three seconds notice of a change.

When deciding what to do in your show, try to structure it to make it entertaining and smooth. Each routine should either run off the previous one or be totally different. Routines you do that require music should be spaced by routines that don't. Skits that require your volunteers standing can be followed by another that doesn't, but never by a third.

Go for high and low shapes in the show, think of how your favourite TV show is framed. Make them deliriously happy then bring them right down to being sad. Give your show contrast and light and shade. This takes experience and a certain amount of understanding of how comedy and pathos work. Remember all stage hypnosis is comedy hypnosis. You are there to make people laugh – to entertain.

One of the best ways of getting tips on delivery and sometimes even routines is not to watch other hypnotists work. Watch comedians, good ones. Get as many videos of your favourite stand up comedians as you can. Watch the comics you can't stand, and watch them incessantly, try to work out why the audience is rolling about when you aren't. Then remember something, your show should make them laugh and feel entertained and try to put your personal view of what's funny to one side. Watch as much theatre as you can in whatever form it takes, and preferably watch it live.

By simple osmosis you'll begin to understand timing, light and shade, structure and how to pull and push your audience.

Back to working script-less. Working with hypnotised volunteers there will always be an element of unpredictability in your show that adds an edge and keeps you on your toes. You can't work to a script in the way a comic or magician can, but then you have the advantage in as much as when things go wrong no one but you know they have, and it's often at these times you get the best laughs! Using your control, off the microphone (I explain this technique in a while) helps here, but there is always the unexpected. I feel that's what makes doing this, so much fun for me.

It helps to be able to ad-lib. I was once working a social club where an older gentleman on stage with me was wearing an ill-fitting pair of dentures, (false teeth). In the original version of this book I declined to say what routine I was doing at the time but now I'll admit that he was imagining he was a vibrator with super power alkaline batteries…needless to say the unpredictable happened and his teeth fell out!

The audience reaction was immense and I played it for all it was worth. The unpredictable became one of the fulcrums and focus for that particular show, and of course those bloody teeth.

First I told him they were not his and try as he might he wouldn't be able to get them back in, then I told him to try and find out who they belonged to. So off he went into the audience shoving them under people's noses much to their disgust and the hilarity of their friends, finally he was told to sell them if he could. He did! We had to buy them back after the show.

I've told you not to milk things, this showbiz term in comedy means doing something ad-nauseam until the audience stops laughing at it, not only a cardinal sin but not very professional. This wasn't so much milking as making use of an unpredictable situation and turning it into a large part of the show that night. I now carry a set of dentures for the odd occasion I can use them.

I can't teach you to 'think on your feet' in this way but never miss an opportunity like this. This is what makes you different. Not props or routines or sets, we all use the same or similar routines. But like an artist the canvas, brushes and paints are the same, it's how you use them that makes the real difference.

1,000,001 ROUTINES

This is an estimate; there could be more. All it takes is a little original thought. That and observation. As I've said I use routines very similar to my colleagues in the business. But hopefully every one has a touch of mine that makes them unique.

I do make, (nothing is really written down unless you count the scribble on the back of a cafe cheque), some of my own up, and so could you.

Just think that everywhere, every day, you are watching potential routines and skits to use on stage, and use that much ignored asset of yours called, inspiration.

I get inspiration from the people watching the shows when they come up to me afterwards and say, "Why didn't you get them to do…"

Television is a great resource for material. Popular programs such as soaps have no idea how their supposedly serious drama can inspire so many sketches for the stage hypnotist. Current films and their stars are another endless supply. Television advertisements are a crock of gold.

I also ask comics what they would do if they were me. They, and that guy down the pub, will have a totally different outlook and approach. But because the guy down the pub has no preconceived ideas or limitations in what the stage offers or hypnosis holds, it's usually him rather than the comic who can come up with the better ideas.

That said there are loads of routines which you will see or hear of being used time and again, the origins of which are lost and the rows about who wrote what, go on forever. As a result, lack of any proper copyright and their usage, means that many can now be considered to be in the public domain, and we list some of them later.

But for those of you who think you have enough creativity to go with your own stuff, I'll give you the basis of all routines and hope you go from there to inspire us all, or better still come up with some so good that the rest of us can't resist stealing them. Remembering that there are no limits to the creativity of your volunteers and that there is also no limit to yours. Be creative and in no time at all you could be heading to 1,000,001 routines.

Change location

I have already mentioned this. Take them somewhere hot, or very cold. Take them somewhere familiar to them such as their work-place, or unfamiliar such as outer space. The trick here is just to take them anywhere outside of the environment they share with you, and the audience, so that they react visually.

Change gender

Have a man behave as a woman, or a woman as a man. For some reason I've discovered that the latter seldom gets a really good audience reaction; whereas turning a man into a woman is for some reason, known only to the audience, hugely funny. This isn't sexist it's an observation, not an opinion.

Change their apparent sexual preference

Be careful here. You may be getting a gay person to hit on another gay person – won't work, no humour. Some people would say that it isn't funny anyway thanks to political correctness which has managed over the last couple of decades to extract the humour from almost anything remotely funny. So to avoid this problem change their sexual preference from human to an inanimate object and then even if their preference goes that way chances are no one will know. I had one guy trying to seduce a fire extinguisher once. He was excellent at it and they are now married and living happily in Milton Keynes. Try it with anything and everything – it's hilarious.

Change sensory perception

There are five physical senses which have predictable results – at least for most of the time. Show a couple of hundred people an apple and they will see an apple. True, Joe Bloggs may see a kumquat but he had a lot of falling over juice the previous evening – or maybe forgot his medication. The results from taste involved with this object, as with smell and texture are normally predictable. Change the result and effect the predictability, and we have a situation that can be hilarious on stage. Let's look at each sense separately. For now I'm not going into details but there is only so many ways you can affect a sense, the rest is cosmetic.

Sight

Make things invisible. The most common items used by all hypnotists are clothing, theirs or the audiences. One of the more common is to turn the focus back onto the person on stage whose movements can be predicted ninety percent of the time...yourself. This results in the good old invisible hypnotist routine. There are a million ways of doing this but there are usually only two reactions, fear and / or curiosity. Knowing that of course you will be careful, done well and with a little imagination, it is definitely a big time routine.

You can also just reverse this effect. Get them to see things that are not there. Pixies, fairies, flying saucers, ghosts, anything, go for it. Just remember to make it visual as well as verbal.

Touch

Make things that are cold feel hot, or hot feel cold: rough, smooth – soft, hard. For instance; use a trigger word and tell them their seat will get red hot every time they hear it. (Safety: make sure you tell them that their skin will not blister or burn., although I've never seen it happen I have no doubt belief can *heal* and also *harm*, so don't let it happen.)

Smell

Most people are not that aware of smell, if they were you'd never see an open car window in a traffic jam. We all know roses smell, but is that good or bad? – remember the reality is your creation. An obvious scenario and very popular in the art, is to tell your volunteers that the other people on stage stink, or smell irresistibly nice and they want to get as close as possible to that smell. Either works well, and is fairly easy to set up.

Taste

Be very careful with this one, as to affect taste it is best to have them put something in their mouths, and that can lead to all sorts of problems.

Obviously you can use fairly safe substances such as a glass of water. Telling them that the water is the most fantastic booze ever made, will illicit two responses, first the expressions of complete bliss when drinking it, second the rather hilarious effects of some-one getting blasted out of their brains on water, slurring their words and if you are lucky bursting into song. Again use caution, not all drunks are happy, so I always tell them they will be.

A really safe one to use with the mouth and I do believe of my own invention, is to get them to find themselves tasty. I usually start with the back of the hand, going on to knees, then elbows. Watch-ing them struggling to try and lick parts of their body they will never reach is hilarious, but always tell them they will not try too hard, or stretch too far. We don't want any pulled muscles. And I know where certain people see this going but for men especially it would require the removal of a couple of vertebrae or an unusual anatomy...

You can, and I have, used other things such as vegetables. The classic is of course the onion routine. Giving them raw onions and telling them that they are eating fruit is a riot. Especially if they believe that only they have the fruit and everyone else is eating horrible smelly onions. However be careful. You do not know these people. For instance who has an ulcer or a hiatus hernia? Who has an allergy to onions? You don't know, but the people with them do, and they do themselves. I am definitely going down on record as saying even though this is the routine I very often end with as my gob-smacker; I am officially telling you not to do this routine.

Hearing

Can you hear me talking right now 'in your head'; of course you can even though you know you can't. Hearing is an easy sense to affect because just as much of it goes on internally as externally, but it's a bugger to get them to react in a way that will resonate with the audience unless you really dress it up. Just cocking their head over to one side with a quizzical expression won't do for any but the most intimate gatherings.

The most common way to do this is to tell them that they can hear anything or anyone – imaginary phone calls from Elvis or God or whoever, can be amazingly funny if you have the right subject, the only problem being that the audience cannot hear what they do, so either take that part yourself or sound with action: 'when you hear 'A', then 'B' will happen.'

Change their persona

You may have a plumber up there with you, a hairdresser or marketing manager and so on. I wonder if you also have a Mel Gibson or a James Bond. Perhaps you are really lucky and have Elvis or even a God or two. Whoever, they are there if you want them to be. Just remember the more inappropriate or different from the volunteer's real life persona, the funnier it will be.

So, we can affect the emotions by adjusting the normal responses to sensual stimuli. In fact that is all we can do.

YOUR PERFORMANCE

Far be it from me to insist that your performance style needs to be anything other than you wish it to be. However, I do have something of a reputation for being a good performer and this comes, or so I believe, from having a solid grounding in showbiz and being lucky enough to have worked beside some consummate professionals.

As with any profession there are accepted ways of doing things, no, not rules, just shared standards. So in this section I'm going to give you pointers which I feel will make your show easier to control, run more smoothly and make your audience happy that they spent good money to come and see you – the real professional – rather than someone who just managed to zap their mate, have bought a karaoke machine and think this makes them a performer.

Being a professional isn't just about whether you make a living from something or not, it's about attitude and doing the best you can regardless of how much you are paid, if at all, or when, where or who you perform for. As all my roadies and assistants will tell you I treat every show as if it were taking place at the London Palladium, Caesars Palace or Sydney Opera House, even if it is actually taking place in The Sprocket and Flange pub. However, these are my opinions and if you want to do it differently go ahead. You have to approach things *your way*.

The first point is never ever try to upstage the stars of a hypnosis show. I know of one guy who stands in the spotlight front of stage all the time throwing suggestions over his shoulder to his hapless 'subjects' who you can't see anyway because he is in the way. Saw another who stands in front of his, asking them questions with his back the audience. As anyone with any stage craft will tell you, you just don't do that except at the most relevant of times, it is rude and it also allows your audiences attention to wonder.

Okay so it's your face and name on the tickets and posters but remember this, people haven't come to see you, they have come to see hypnosis. They have not come to see your new suit, your wonderful smile or the cute way you have of tipping your head to one side. They have come to see people on stage (preferably their friends and family) making fools of themselves at your command. Were anything else true then you wouldn't need the rest of this book because you wouldn't need ten or twelve volunteers and an idea of how to zap them. The true stars of any hypnosis show are the people you get up on stage.

After it's all done and you've got them their applause and returned them to their friends and families, you can take your bow. Don't try and lecture them or advertise any hypnosis tapes you may be selling. Use dead spots in the show for this. Usually it is a waste of time anyway for as soon as your friends return to their seats the questions will start.

"What did it feel like?" "Do you remember anything?" Etc.

You will be wasting your time trying to battle against this so don't take too long in saying your farewells. Wish them goodnight and get off. You will have an opportunity to wallow in some glory if you hang around afterwards in the bar selling some merchandise, answering questions, making yourself available. Few performers do this, which is really stupid. It's a huge PR exercise and can get you bookings for everything from weddings to funerals (we've all 'died' on stage). I always do it. I am almost always the last person to leave the venue. It also helps in case anyone is still feeling the 'effects' to be on hand to reassure them and correct any 'hypnotic hangovers', which shouldn't happen but, we can and do make mistakes.

In my humble opinion a good stage hypnotist will get them up, get them 'under' and, apart from when delivering suggestions, should virtually become invisible.

If you are working an area with no room behind their chairs, which you shouldn't be if you've taken control when you got there, then unless otherwise absolutely necessary, stand at the side of the stage. In the first few routines it's important that you see their faces to check for the points we mentioned earlier and to assess which are the most expressive, you can do that easily from here. After this try not to get between your friends on stage and your audience, unless it's part of a routine.

I work behind the chairs. Being behind them makes life simpler anyway, allowing you to be right up close at the delivery of a suggestion meant for a single individual. You can then place your hand lightly on their shoulder and say, "I'm talking to the person I am touching now. When you open your eyes…" then tell them what it is you want them to do. That way you can make sure that they understand the suggestion, usually by asking them to nod if they do, and are close enough to confirm the state of hypnosis by looking for the telltale blush and muscle flaccidity.

Unless you can sing superbly, dance like Fred Astair or tell jokes as well as a comic, then don’t do any of these things. For the majority of the show try to be more of a compere and master of ceremonies, than a front man.

CONTROLLING REACTION

For most of the time you are quite safe allowing the volunteers to react to your suggestions spontaneously. However, on occasion you will need a specific act to take place to get your 'belly laugh'. Never leave this to chance. Remember that with music playing, laughter and all the other 'white noise' in the venue, the audience can only hear you over the microphone. The hypnotised volunteers however are right up close and they can hear every word. Working 'off mic.' can make your act ten times funnier and give far more control than you would otherwise have. I constantly talk to my volunteers off the microphone. I increase their reactions if they are not going for it enough. I give extra suggestions and tell them exactly what to do. Now I am no ventriloquist but I don't have to be – no one is watching me! I have never had anyone apart from fellow hypnotists even notice what I'm doing. Even then, rarely.

Magicians use misdirection constantly. They will bring the audiences attention to one hand while the other is doing something devious behind their line of sight. You already have the world's greatest misdirection. Your audience's attention is firmly focused on your volunteers. Nobody will notice you talking quietly to him or her in the background. For instance, you have two people arguing over ownership of a pixie. You have already told them that they will not get violent, just in case, and they are squabbling quite nicely but you need a full-blown row! Drop your microphone towards them, your audience needs to hear them anyway, and quietly begin to control the situation.

"He's pissing you off. God she's making you angry." Phrases like this can add so much to an otherwise banal situation.

They'll respond to this automatically but be careful. They will tend to repeat any profanities. Fine if you have an adult audience and you want them to do that. I sometimes do just this and then 'punish' them for being so rude by telling them to stick their tongue out and then suggesting it's stuck there. With their tongue out I then interview them and the resulting spluttering and attempts to speak properly are extremely funny. Don't do this if it's a family show – only you can be the judge of that.

Using this method of constantly giving suggestions off the microphone is how I make my shows predictable – for me – and superbly controllable.

PROPS

You already have these: your volunteers.

I have seen everything from tiny dolls to huge spacecraft used on stage. Why bother? The funniest thing you can do is to get them to react inappropriately to everyday articles. We've all seen the guy hitting on what he believes is a beautiful girl, when in actual fact it's a mop or a broom. What venue doesn't have these things?

I do carry a small suitcase containing a few inflatable toys, a blow up skeleton for the invisible hypnotist routine for example. I also have a telephone with a microphone in it for talking to God or Elvis, a hand puppet chimpanzee called Charlie and on occasion have been known to carry some vegetables. But besides that 'specialist' props are just an unnecessary complication, unless your imagination is sadly lacking.

Also consider the safety angle again. Props are just one more potential accident waiting to happen. Why make your life difficult?

START BIG FINISH BIGGER

We all know the old show business axiom, start small finish big. In other words being laid back at the start and building step by step to a huge ending. What a load of rubbish that is. Okay may be for some acts or shows but not for the comedy hypnosis show.

Watch the truly great comics. They hit them where it hurts from gag one. They will start with really strong material and end with strong material. Anything new, or their weaker gags, will be spaced out in the middle. You should do the same.

You have already started very dramatically if you've used the drop back, if not make sure that your first few routines, although easy for your volunteers imaginations to handle, always get good audience response. To let you into a secret here, audiences prefer the less complicated stuff, and so do I. The suggestions are faster and the reactions are usually bigger. Don't fall into the trap of thinking that if you spend a fortune on props, lighting and music, that it will make your act better in some way.

Don't do the intellectual bit. Look at the most popular types of television programmes throughout the world, soaps! People don't want to think when being entertained so keep it simple!

Any new routines you are adding, or routines that you don't yet have a replacement for, but know are fairly weak, you put in the middle, preferably between really strong ones. That way you can start big and finish bigger!

My final tip here comes from one of Britain's most successful comics of all time. He is surprisingly little known outside of the UK but doesn't care as he fills theatres up and down these islands every week and has been making a very nice living for over 60 years in the biz. His name is Ken Dodd.

The Ken Dodd tip.

"If it's worth a minute, give it thirty seconds."

That has made my shows so much sharper, snappier and funnier. True you have to have a huge bag full of routines but never ever milk it until your audience stops laughing. Get the roar, the belly laugh and quickly go on to the next one. Milking is the old way of doing things and will soon get you the reputation of being boring.

More importantly it will get THE HYPNOTIST the reputation of being boring so . . . Don't do it.

ASSISTANTS

I suppose the question is do you need them? And the answer is, of course, no. Most performers don't and that results in empty chairs being left on stage – or worse you are seen to be moving them yourself – it results in breaks and fumbles searching for props or having to be in the right place at the right time when some volunteer is in precisely the wrong one at the wrong time.

My personal view is yes, have and use assistants, or at the very least assistant. If not on stage then off as a roadie or road manager, depending on how much you want to pay them. At least have someone there to turn your music on at the right time.

The main difference between looking like a pro and coming across as a fumbling amateur is appearing to be 'professional', and a real professional to my mind will not do the menial tasks themselves.

This is a contentious stance for all those performers who think it's the done thing to fiddle about with the remote control for a mini-disc or MP3 player, or worse a tape deck or CD. Besides the fact that the audience do notice, no matter what you think, it does take your focus away from your friends on stage, no matter how ambi-dextrous you think your mind is.

An assistant also has other uses, such as helping to spot fakers and adding to routines, as you have another foil with which to thrust a joke at, without ridiculing your volunteers too much.

MAKING MONEY

I've been asked to include in this book some ideas for actually making a living from the art of stage hypnosis. This isn't as easy to write as it first seems, as one of the largest barriers to becoming the star hypnotist is that – unlike outer space – there is so much room in the showbizasphere. And given that this book is not being sold solely aiming at the UK market, we have to understand that there are so many differences in entertainment culture between say the UK and the USA.

For instance American high schools often have shows for the students and PTA's, the UK doesn't get close to this until university level, unless you count 'Under Milk Wood' which almost all of us parents have to sit through at least once.

The UK had a tradition of working men's social clubs attended by families to watch variety shows and the American's have show bars. Although the UK club scene is less than busy now.

This is only the very tip of the iceberg when it comes to differences, however some concepts are hopefully inspiring and action provoking wherever you live and work, so here goes.

Publicity:

Spend some real cash. Photographs should be professionally done. Design and printing should be top notch and the whole package should smell so much of star that passing UFO's detour to avoid burn-up. Your publicity package is your shop front, sides and back. Keep it updated and slick. It's worth every penny. In today's world of multimedia, include good show reels, of about three to five minutes and make them fast and funny.

AGENTS

Showbiz agents tend to be everywhere. Like cockroaches they will probably survive the nuclear holocaust. Thank god.

A good agent is a wonderful thing; bringing you contacts you'd rarely otherwise make and taking all the business out of show business. That said not every agent is good and a bad one is terrible. So how do you know?

Here's a hot tip. Research the area you'd like to work. Initially look up the yellow pages or business directory – do not use the Internet as anyone with a brain cell can look like a decent set up on a web page. At least the yellows show that they have also spent money, and will mean they will spend cash to find you and your peers some work.

Ring them up and pretend to be a punter looking for a hypnotist and see if they can get one easily and if so, who.

A friend of mine used to run a bit of a scam on this theme that helped establish him at the time. He's gone on now so I'll let you in on this; just don't tell anyone as this is gorilla marketing at its best.

Get several friends to ring an agent who isn't aware of you. They pretend they are bar or club or venue owners looking for this fabulous hypnotist named *insert your name here*. When the agent offers them someone else they insist emphatically that they want you – telling them they went on some sort of trip with a group of other organisers or whatever, helps. By the time they get your publicity the agent is bating for you – they can smell a commission from three continents away.

Now it is of course possible not to use agents. Most top names don't. They have managers, that is someone who costs way more than the agent but is totally devoted to bleeding you dry, sorry, scratch that and replace with totally devoted to guiding your career to the heights. It should be noted that this is tinged with a British eye view. In the US the gap between agent and manager is less discernable but in both cases they tend to find you by reputation or sheer chance, or by the fact that every lamp post in their street has your posters on it, the postman shoves your un-enveloped flyers in the mailbox every morning as he plans what to do with the small gratuity he found himself with. Go for it, it's the easiest way to get on but, and I can't emphasise this too strongly, you'd better be good because if you let just one down, the rest will know before you have said sorry.

SELF promotion:

There are lots of ways where you can play the roles of director, producer, promoter and performer, here are a few, some are time, labour and financially costly and some as easy as going on holiday, but at some time they have all worked for someone, even me.

The important thing to remember is that every opportunity to promote yourself, and your name, should not be missed. Take something with you wherever you go and learn that if you are 'out' then whoever is entertaining you or giving you a service could be a source of business.

Restaurants do birthday parties or may even cater outside for larger events.

Taxis take all sorts of people to and from venues; a good tip and a handful of info cards can get you some very nice business.

Hotels with function and conference suites: Approach the manager and suggest they could offer a complete package of room and entertainment for corporate clients. For this approach get together with maybe a band or singer, maybe also a travelling DJ and work on a full evening's package.

Hairdressers do wedding packages as do wedding shops, and the wedding organisers will possibly have never thought of hypnosis as a different style of entertainment for the reception, did you? I've done lots, and a usual skit of mine is to tell the groom, if I'm lucky enough to get him, that when I wake him up he will not get an erection for the next two weeks; then charge the bride for taking that one away.

Pubs in the UK are always looking for anything that will get punters in and unlike many of the more established performers who tend to look down on working in tiny spaces to a handful of people in less than salubrious conditions, I suggest you do as many as possible. I've had some of my best experiences on these nights and being up close and personal with the audience really keeps you on your toes.

The easiest way to get these venues is to go for a drink. Ten minutes after getting in the place have someone stuck to the bar – staff preferably, but not the landlord – and have a pocket full of cards. Nothing sells you better than hypnosis itself.

Hire a small venue – village hall – rehearsal rooms – function room – town hall. Pick a small community and find out where the local amateur dramatics association or even the scouts and guides put their shows on and hire that.

In a small place the cost of publicity is reduced. Local shops, petrol stations, even bars if you offer them a free seat, will display your posters for free and if the local 'entertainment' can fill the place, so can you.

There are several world renown performers who started this way and rose to hiring theatres, which is more costly but in reality no harder.

Have a couple of posters mounted on boards and stick these on the verge of the two or three roads leading into the place.

DJ's can be a good supply of income. As can any other performer; unless it's another hypnotist, you don't clash with anyone. I spent a few good years going on the road with a girl singer who also acted as my assistant. The package was excellent and only needed one set of PA gear and one roadie.

SOUND AND LIGHTING

Microphone mastery and visual delights

Getting the sound of your voice and music absolutely right is of paramount importance. It is for this reason that I insist you get a good roadie or assistant.

Even after you sound check, unless you are working a venue where your speakers are behind you in which case unless its extremely small, you have set up badly; you need someone out there who can hear what you can't.

I never trust anyone to initially set my sound, I do it. I get my radio mic and go to the back of the venue as far away from the speakers as possible. I first set the tone of my voice and gain or pick up off the mic. You are listening for clarity here. Your voice should sound crisp and clear.

Too much bottom or bass and you'll sound as if you are wearing a gag, too much top or treble and you're doing smurf impressions. On most average systems a setting of halfway on these is best and just adjust your middle to get your voice sounding just as it does normally, but louder.

Next set your mic gain. The higher the gain the further from your mouth you can hold it. The important thing here is to remember that you will undoubtedly have your volunteers talk at some point. They will anyway whether you want them to or not and most of the time what they say will need to be heard. To do this it's best to point your mic at them without having to shove it up their nostrils to hear anything. I shudder when I see this simple thing done badly, and it often is. If you ask them a question point the mic at them, and wait until they have actually answered the question before taking it away. I once watched a Hypnotist asking questions and just repeating what his volunteer said, never once could you hear if the guy actually said what the hypnotist was repeating. The audience tittered where they would have guffawed, the volunteers timing was way better then the hypnotists.

You must also remember that volunteers are usually even less used to using and handling a microphone than you are. They will not speak clearly. They will mumble, stumble, spit and sometimes shout, (Tip: Don't let them sneeze on your mic it will bugger the head)] they are not holding the thing and you are. If you are working this professionally, and by professional I'm referring to attitude not whether you are doing it full time, then get some practise in with a microphone and watch how really good pros use one. Not doing so, or just thinking anyone can do this, is both painfully amateur and very stupid.

I wouldn't do a Britney here and get one of those over the ear jobs or a leveller or tie clip. It's not easy to talk off it, and it really is hard to use with your volunteers as you'd look as if you were trying to French kiss them every time you needed to get it close. Whatever you do don't use two, that's just another thing to handle and another thing to go wrong. Keep it simple. Use a good quality hand held with fresh nicam batteries every time. If you use cheap you'll sound cheap.

Now back to the back of room and setting your music. I don't care how pertinent you feel your carefully chosen orchestral piece is to the event, it should never be louder than your mic. The exceptions being your introduction and walk off music. If anything untoward should happen during a ballet dance routine or something happens to your Elvis impersonator – yes for some reason people still do that one (shrugs) – over the other side of the stage you must be heard over the music.

Besides which the audience haven't paid to hear the music, the volunteers couldn't hear an anvil drop if genuinely hypnotised unless told to do so, and backing music should be just that, back, way back. Just take a look at TV and films and notice how even though the music is there, it is very understated.

If you have never worked with sound before and are setting up your own gear here are a few pointers.

Work behind your speakers. This cuts the possibility of that high whine we know of as feedback. Set up a fold-back speaker or monitor. Usually one small speaker set just loud enough so that you and your volunteers can hear everything clearly on stage. Set your main speakers as high and as far apart as possible. If working a square shaped room set them at an angle so that a straight line drawn from them out into the room would cross at a point roughly one third of the rooms length away from the back wall. Set your sound engineer at the centre back of the room if possible.

On the odd occasion I've worked 'L' shaped rooms. Here set two speakers, one to serve one angle of the room, the other pointing down the other. It's not ideal but it works.

I always endeavour to sound check before any paying punters arrive. This however isn't always possible and when it isn't you can turn it to your advantage. I never have any music played that I will be using in the show but just get something I know is recorded at the same level as my show stuff. Whilst that is playing I'll sound check, starting off with the mandatory, "One. One two. One. Icicles, Bicycles, Testi . . . one, one two three." This gets me my first laugh. I'll then follow this with, "Listening only to the sound of my voice and feeling very sleepy and relaxed..." Ask anyone there if they can hear you and regardless of the answer smile mischievously and say, "Oh good". After a while you'll pick out one or two who will go from this.

Lighting

I'm assuming here you are working in a situation where the lighting is adjustable, as in a really good club or a theatre. Outside of this just get as much as you can.

I always again set my own lights and take from me it's best not to use effects. They may make the stage or you look very good but the really important thing is that your audience is able to see the facial expressions of your volunteers.

Now this is normally no problem for a professional cast and lighting crew. This is because all of the cast are wearing 'slap' and have eye-liner and blusher, lipstick and powder on. So on stage or indeed even more so on TV, the abnormal is normal. Think of this then, your volunteers will either be wearing no powder and paste or way the wrong sort, put on inexpertly – for the stage that is. Light your stage with too much blue and some will look as if they have seen several ghosts and the rest will look as if they are ghosts. Light it too red and they'll look – especially if they suffer with hypnotic blush – as if they have just had hard sex. Light it too yellow and the jaundice monster will rise. Just use white light. It serves the purpose of allowing your audience to see clearly. Never use a spotlight as they are okay when the operator knows where the hell the person is going, and have the house lights turned up if you are sending people out into the audience or working with them there.

I always get someone to sit on the chairs on stage and then go as far away as possible. I then tell them to show me only facial expressions for sad, mad, happy, whatever. With my eyesight, if I can see them clearly then just about every one else can.

Finally if my own roadie isn't handling things directly I remind the sound and lighting guys or gals that if anything goes wrong or changes, that I will ensure that the rest of there lives will not be worth living as they will spend it believing they are ducks.

Rehearsing

You can of course rehearse microphone technique. Use a recording device and get a friend to be your volunteer. Set it up as if on stage with you standing and them sitting or whatever.

You'll have no problem finding out if your gags work down the local bar, and anyone who'll stand still long enough can become your testing ground to see if your technique works.

Rehearsing a whole show however isn't always that easy because you need an independent audience from which to gather your volunteers and your feedback.

There is however a way you can do this and build your reputation at the same time. Charity shows and fundraisers.

Just pick a charity or an organisation locally who needs funds and go offer them a totally free show. Not only will you be able to get good guy promotional material from such an event, you can try out new stuff and gain that all important experience without having to worry about not being paid.

The organisation will find the venue, advertise you, sell your tickets and wipe your fevered brow. You'll ask nicely of the audience if it's okay if you try out some new stuff on them and remind them that they are there to support a good cause, not to be entertained, which might happen anyway.

All the pressure is then off you apart from delivering hypnosis, and even then if you don't you can convince yourself it was because they were there because of the good cause, and so it wasn't your fault they didn't want hypnosis.

I know of some really long time pros who still use this type of show to try out new routines or to invite potential future bookers to come and get a taste of them, it's a total win win situation and gives you a great buzz.

CAN IT GO WRONG?

No matter how carefully you prepare, plan and check, things can still go wrong. At least that is how it will look to the outside observer. Fortunately the worst of these are predictable and therefore easily prepared for.

For instance, think – some people when laughing a lot can lose control of their bladder, the same with crying and being *SHIT* scared. Vomiting is a common reaction to things smelling or tasting bad or awful. You have no idea what might make someone aggressive, unless your suggestion is aimed at producing just that effect. A simple caveat to your suggestion of "You will not have an accident", "You will not be sick" and of course "You will not hit, punch, kick, bite, throw anything at or in any way molest the HYPNOTIST!" All of these have the two fold effect of keeping things safe and getting an extra laugh from the audience, to say nothing of increasing their believability with your volunteers.

ABREACTION

Occasionally, and I do really mean occasionally as this has happened to me three times out of thousands, you may come across what psychologists and psychotherapists call an 'abreaction' happening spontaneously to one of your friends on stage. This is the emotional response to a full blown re-living of an event in the person's past. No, not a memory but really re-experiencing it. It's so real to them that if physical harm was involved wheals and bruises have been know to re-occur. I have seen this but only ever in consultation. It's also of note that abreactions are not always 'bad'. The emotions can be laughter as well as tears.

I was once asked how to deal with this and to be honest if you do your intro carefully, induce well and phrase your suggestions well, the problem should never arise. Although anyone can spontaneously abreact at any time, it just needs a trigger, they shouldn't if you are in full control of the situation and have them fully focused on your given reality – or hypnotised but – sometimes your attention slips. If it does happen dealing with it is simple.

It would be inappropriate to deal with what could be a case of childhood abuse or another issue on stage, and bloody hard as well with everything else going on, so here is how to get out quick – get them out of it quickly. Firmly command that this is not the time or place, reassure them that you will speak with them after the show and so they need not bring these memories back with them, and do a wake up.

You may struggle a little as they may not want to let go until the issue is sorted, if that's so have a look at the (sleepers below) and use one of the more forceful wake up routines.

SLEEPERS

If you do your wake up properly, you will not get the problem of what we call in the business, a 'sleeper'. Unfortunately it happens.

A sleeper is that odd creature who won't wake up after a show. Rarely it's because they are a dick-head who hasn't been hypnotised at all and is trying to make you look a fool. If you haven't noticed them already, then you deserve them. We'll deal with them in a moment.

The reasons people become a 'sleeper' is that they have a life style, or a job, which is stressful, fraught, or are just too busy to relax. This is possibly the first time in years they've felt so good, so calm, so relaxed, so leaving this nice restful place in their head is not on and you can go hang when you count five! They are staying put! Oh no they're not!

Nine times out of ten you can spot a potential sleeper, their reactions to your suggestions have been lethargic or non-existent. Pay them special attention during your wake up. If however they still refuse to wake up it's very simple to get them to do so. Do this off mic. Whisper in their ear or else all the work you've just done making yourself appear to be a wonderful and caring person, will fly straight out of the window!

Say to them:

"I'm going to count one to five. On the count of five you will open your eyes and feel wonderful. This wonderful calm will stay with you and you will feel great like this for a long, long time. If you don't wake up when I reach the number five and open your eyes you will get the worst headache you've ever had and it could last for days."

Ask them now on the microphone to nod their head if they understand. Then quickly count from one to five and almost shout 'wide awake.' In all my years doing it this has never failed. If it does it's because you have not made the threat clear enough. Use any threat you like, toothache etc, but remember not to use anything that could cause real harm or it could just bounce back to you.

It was once suggested, by a friend after a show, that when I had a sleeper I should carry a hatpin with me. The premise being that if suggestion didn't work then the pin would! With the faker it probably would. But he may be bigger than you and carry a mean punch.

It goes without saying that you should never deliberately injure your friends on stage.

Finally a friend of mine Barry Thain uses a less commanding and more co-operative approach - "I know you are very happy right now but if you don't come out when I tell you, you will never be able to return to this lovely feeling." "It works very well, and has fewer potential problems that threatening someone, who may suffer migraines, with a headache."

I have to say I've never had anyone with a headache; the point is they want to avoid such.

FAKERS

You will get them. Very occasionally they will come on stage to pretend to be hypnotised and to make you look ridiculous. They may even have an ambulance-chasing lawyer in tow! Look for the tell tale signs of their friends giggling at inappropriate times, especially when you have your back turned to them. By far the easiest way of spotting them is to have a Roadie or assistant to do the looking for you and signal you. You shouldn't miss them but it can happen so easily with everything else that you have to think about.

The other variety of 'faker' you will sometimes get, are those who genuinely wanted to be hypnotised but didn't make it, and because your opening patter was so good they truly believe that if they don't go 'under' then they must be stupid and don't want anyone to know. So rather than face the embarrassment of going back to their friends unsuccessful they stay with you and pretend.

The first type of faker, get rid of immediately, but remember you are in control. They have already had a few giggles from their friends and you have to turn that situation around or you will end up with a full-blown omelette on your face. I single them out and do a few special 'tests' on them. Anything you can think of that makes them look as ridiculous as possible. I then say something like, "You haven't gone you know, so I think it would be best if you go," then immediately turn to the audience and get them a round of applause for being a good sport or something. Don't try to get your own back too much unless you have a couple of minders with you and a fast car waiting outside. This is his hometown, not yours, and car parks at the end of business can often be likened to the final frontier.

The second faker is much easier to deal with. For a start they will do virtually everything you ask them to. Often they will be even better than those who are 'genuinely' hypnotised. They tend to go right over the top as they see this as the only way of avoiding getting 'caught out'. Use them. Let them do what they do. Let them get laughs and make fools of themselves. That is what the audience wants to see. I know this sounds like I am telling you to cheat but there has to have been occasions where every hypnotist has had this type of faker on stage and have even missed it themselves, or at least been unsure as to their state. So what? The whole business of stage hypnosis is to entertain a paying audience, nothing more. If you go out with the idea that you have to prove hypnosis in anyway you are on a very slippery slope with no safety line.

On the odd occasion where you have a good faker who is getting reactions from the audience and you have no doubt that they are faking; still use them. The opportunity here to show off and make yourself look amazing shouldn't be missed. Chances are that if you know they are faking then so does half your audience, or at the very least they will suspect that the guy third from the left doesn't look hypnotised. Fine, keep them there for the whole show and then, when you are about to get your volunteers their applause; pull your faker to the front first. I put my arm around their shoulders and say something like, "well Jon, (Fred, Jill, whatever) you've been here the whole show and you've done everything haven't you? The thing is I know you haven't gone. They know you haven't gone, don't you feel a fool?"

Then I immediately turn to the audience and say,

"Ladies and gentlemen it takes a lot of guts to come up here and be silly while you are hypnotised, it takes a lot more to do it when you aren't. Please give --- a huge round of applause for being so brave!"

Why do this? Because it gets rid of any embarrassment for the poor soul when they rejoin their friends and makes you look like a damn good sport. It will probably get you a couple of free drinks after the show as well. But most importantly it shows you actually do know what you are supposed to be doing.

INSURANCE

As much as you can afford. Public liability and Professional Indemnity insurance is available and is an absolute necessity for anyone dealing with the public. Do not try and save money on this and make absolutely sure that it covers you as a Hypnotist.

Note: now that the European Human Rights Bill is fully in force in the UK, take my advice and double your insurance. This bill makes it incredibly easy for everyone to sue everyone else for just about anything.

Also make a point of ensuring that it states quite clearly in your contract that your insurance only comes into force when the state of hypnosis is a direct cause of harm or injury. Should the cause of any such harm or injury be the state of repair of the stage or any equipment supplied by the venue then it is the venue that is responsible for any claims made.

Stage hypnosis insurance is not easy to get but the Academy of Hypnotic Arts does have a resource for procuring a worldwide insurance; the contact details can be found at the back of the book.

IMPROMPTU HYPNOSIS

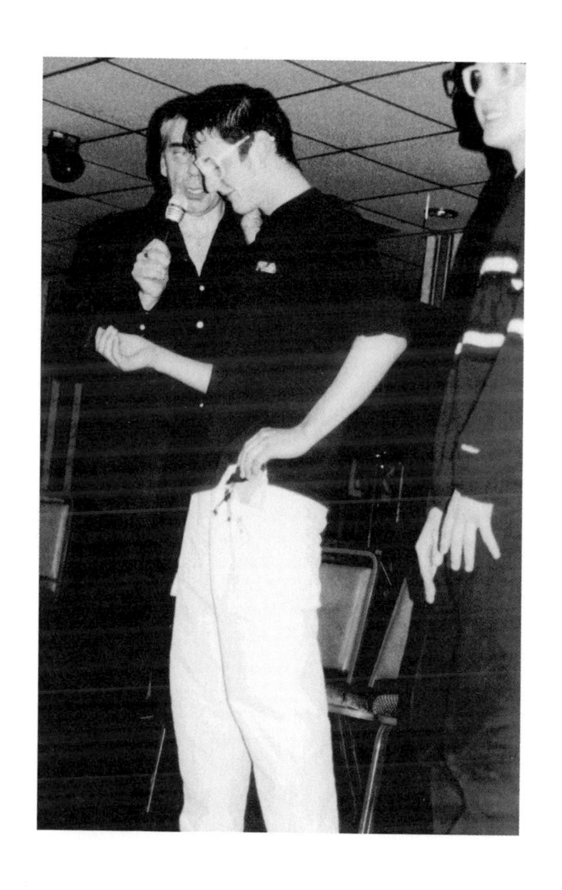

This is, as I have said, by far the most opportune moment to both rehearse and promote yourself. Take full advantage of it.

The occasion will arise when people find out what you do, the question, “Could you hypnotise me?” will be asked. Unless there is a reason you cannot accept this ‘challenge’ such as being on your way out of the door to catch a train or flight, take the challenge! It will be a reputation builder and is a fabulous opportunity to practise. I have got some of my most inspired ideas for routines doing my thing at parties and just having an evening out. Often I’ve also turned these occasions into paid bookings.

For this I usually use my version of the Dave Elman eye closure induction, as this is by far the easiest in these circumstances. Sit them down and tell them to close their eyes.

You:

“Now pretend, just imagine that your eyes won’t open, and when you’re positive, when you are absolutely certain that your eyes won’t open, test them.”

What should happen now is that you will see them lifting their eyebrows and really struggling to get their eyes open. Sometimes of course they will just open them. When this happens say:

"No, I said to test that your eyes won't open – you're testing that they will and we all know they will open, now let's test that they won't. Try again."

Repeat the first part and more often than not, I have a 99.9999~% success rate with this, they won't be able to open them. Now remember the big secret of the stage hypnotist that if they will accept one suggestion, they'll accept them all. Say to them, "Great, and if you can relax the eyelids to the point where you can't open them you can relax your whole body and mind."

Now use the deepening procedure. In this situation I test their compliance with suggestion by having them lock their hands in a tight fist and tell them that when they open their eyes and look at their hands they won't be able to straighten the fingers. Also tell them that this will be funny, or they may become concerned, and as soon as you have success with this one then you are away. If you are quick you can also make the other hand into a fist and be amazed at how funny it is watching someone trying to lift up a glass, or anything else, with fists instead of hands.

Now, even though this is impromptu I'd suggest that you 'set your stage'. Just move your friend to another chair pulled just a little away from the watching crowd. Or just pull them away. Setting an area for performance like this, and that is what we mean by stage in this case, allows you more control and makes the volunteer feel more detached. Painting a picture for their psyche can help as well. (I usually do this under different circumstances with lots of lights, a big stage, microphone, huge audience.) Finally, always use the full waking procedure no matter where you are.

HINTS AND TIPS

The following hints and tips are all based on my opinion or experience.

Quality not quantity. Don't worry how many subjects you have. Give me three good ones rather than twelve so-so, every time. On the odd occasion I've worked with one, usually at parties and impromptu in bars. A good hypnotist can get at least forty minutes out of one subject before it begins to look like you are 'picking' on them.

Tidy your stage. If you start with twelve chairs but only get seven or eight subjects, get rid of the empty chairs. Audiences will count them but not the subjects. It could be considered a mark of failure so get rid of them.

Be 'THE Hypnotist' from the second you enter the venue to the second you leave.

Always make sure everyone hypnotised is happy and well after the show. Stick around and be there to sort any problems. There shouldn't be any but we are all capable of making mistakes.

Give your volunteers a gift. In Britain we are not allowed to pay them – thank the Gods. The best thing I've found is to give them free tickets to your next show in their area. Not only will you have someone you know who will be hypnotisable next time round, but also they will bring with him or her, others who are emotionally primed to volunteer.

Always be knowledgeable. Answer all questions before and after a show. Never admit you don't know the answers to the public. If in doubt, bullshit. It is after all what you do. Then immediately do some research and find the answer for the next time you get asked.

Always take care that your show cannot in any way rebound on you in any aspect. If you look after yourself you will have to look after your friends on stage.

Never lend, show or give anyone a copy of this book. Steps will be taken.

Remember you can never fail. If for some reason you attempt to hypnotise someone and they don't go it's because they are not in the right mood, or have had too much to drink. One of my favourites is to tell them that they are trying too hard. But it is always their fault not yours. Just don't make an enemy by telling them that they are too stupid to be hypnotised, even if you believe this to be the case.

If you 'lose' a subject in the middle of a show, they will stop responding and probably tell you they have had enough, don't worry. Get rid of them as smoothly as possible. However, I always tell them that I would like them to join me on stage at the end of the show and put them through the wake up procedure. Not only does this get rid of any chance of a hypnotic hangover but also once again it shows you are the concerned professional you truly are.

Rehearsing. You can't. At least not in the way any other act can. Sure you can run through the way you deliver your opening and gags, even the way you deliver suggestions but unless you have a bunch of willing friends who are happy to let you practise on them you've struck out. In most cases if your friends knew you before you became a hypnotist you will have a hell of a job convincing them you can do it. The best opportunity you will have to try your skills will be in impromptu circumstances. That's why I've given that subject its own section, but you can get some show practice where you have an audience and willing volunteers where it doesn't matter so much if your show isn't the complete success it will be in the future. Wherever you are in the world there are always charities and organisations desperately trying to raise funds. Approach them and offer your services. Give them a show for free but get them to pay for any advertising and printing costs. They get their funds; you get your rehearsal and experience. It's a win – win situation and if you do well, these organisations will be only too happy to provide you with a letter of recommendation that you can use in your publicity.

Be flexible. It is impossible for you to predict how many volunteers you will have or what gender and age they might be. If you figure ten or fifteen routines can get you through an hours show make sure you have twenty or thirty just in case.

Stooges. Don't use them. There have been those in the past who have turned up at venues with their own retinue of 'volunteers' following in a bus. They always get caught out eventually destroying their own and everyone else's reputations for a while.

Have a good time and let it show. If you are enjoying the show I can guarantee your audience will.

THE ROUTINES

This is a list of routines for you to use in your show. Some of them work better with music; some are more effective in cabaret than in theatre. All of them are workable sometime, somewhere. I do not lay claim for the general ideas here but have re-written these over the years to fit my style. You should do the same. Remember that the trick is to make things simple for your subjects and fast and funny for your audience.

Alien

You are an alien from another planet; you can't speak earth language just your own, which is very strange. Now tell the person next to them that they understand every word and get them to interpret.

Ancient

Tell them that on waking they are all becoming very, very old, absolutely ancient. In the right circumstances tell one of the guys that he is the world's dirtiest and oldest, dirty old man. (Not sure of my American here. Dirty in this context in Britain means lascivious).

Anti-hypnosis

Pick one or two. Tell them that they hate stage hypnosis. Tell them they think that anyone who can be hypnotised is foolish, weak-willed etc. Tell them that they are sitting next to people who have been hypnotised. Control the situation so that they begin to get upset with you.

Astronaut

Tell them that they are astronauts out in space and are becoming weightless.

Baby burps

Get them to burp a baby and tell them that when they hear the burp, do this yourself, that stuff will begin coming from both ends of the baby all over them.

Balance

Have them put both arms out level with the shoulders. Tell them whichever arm you push down the other will shoot up.

Beautiful people

Tell all the guys that they are Miss World and get them to throw everyone kisses and walk around displaying how beautiful they are. Tell the girls that they are Mr. Universe.

Birthing

Tell the guys they are in the last stages of labour. Interview a good one and ask him how it happened.

Blind date

Split them into couples. Ignore gender. Tell them they are on a blind date with the person next to them. Depending on the mix, you be the judge, tell them their date partner is lousy or wonderful.

Bra flies

Tell them that every time you touch your shoulder or chin, or scratch your knee, the girls will notice that their bra catch has broken and the guys will notice their zipper / flies are open.

Break free

Do this sitting or standing: standing is funnier. Tell them that one of their feet is stuck to the floor, or that they can't get up because they are stuck to the chair. Being careful to tell them that they will not have any accidents, now tell them they need to go to the bathroom, badly.

Cartoon pals

Tell them that they have a famous cartoon character sitting next to them.

Cell shoe

Tell all of the subjects that they are expecting a very important call on their cell phone, which has been secretly embedded into their shoe. (Have the sound of a mobile phone played.)

Changing names

Get a couple of subjects. Girl/boy or boy/boy works best. Tell the first one that their name is something ridiculous. If it's a guy tell him his name is Abigail. If a girl then her name is Theodore, or something. Now tell the guy that's left that he finds the other's name, laugh out loud funny. Then whisper that when you ask him his name it has changed to Tinkerbelle and that he gets defensive, but not violent, when people think it's funny. If you have the time and the recall to remember lots of inappropriate names then you can use more than two people. The names people call their pets are wonderful for this. Do it early on and leave it in until the end and call them by their new names.

Coming out

Pick an obviously heterosexual subject and tell them they have decided to 'come out' and tell their friends and family in the audience they are gay. Then tell them there is someone on the front row they really fancy and to use body language to 'pick them up'.

Dancers

Tell them they are the world's greatest dancers. Tell them that they can do any style of dance from disco to ballet and that when the music starts they will interpret the music to the best of their abilities. Have some disco music played for about 1 minute then change to a ballet piece from Swan Lake or something.

Dandruff obsession

Tell them they will realise that they have a dandruff obsession and that they must brush it off, even from other people's shoulders. In cabaret send them out into the audience, otherwise keep them on stage and tell them everyone has a huge dandruff problem.

Drill Sergeant

Tell a guy he is the drill sergeant. The other subjects or the audience are the worst recruits he has ever seen. If you have the right girl make her a sergeant who thinks they all look wonderful. Control an argument between the sergeants.

Elbow Doctor

Tell them they are a world famous elbow Doctor and that they will walk around and inspect people's elbows to make sure they bend correctly.

Finger stuck

Tell them that when they wake they will have an itch in their right ear. Tell them to gently put their finger in there and give it a scratch, but, the finger sticks and the only way to get it unstuck is to put their other index finger up their nose. Guess what, that sticks and the only way to get it out is to stick their other index finger back in the ear and guess what…

Fleas

Tell them they have fleas on their knees, then on their bodies and finish with their posterior. (Just a note: In Britain we use the word 'bum' to describe the derrière, the word 'fanny' describes a woman's reproductive organs and as such you have to be careful!)

Flies

Tell them that the place is full of flies buzzing around their heads.

Force field

Tell all subjects of the opposite sex they are madly in lust with you. Tell them they want to touch you, but there is a force field all around your body and they cannot get you. Drop the force field only if you dare.

Forget how old

Tell them they can't remember how old they are. Tell them to guess and that the figure is probably somewhere between six and ninety two.

Forget how to add

Tell them they can't remember how to add numbers. Tell them that whatever numbers you give them the answer will always be seven hundred and sixty eight.

Forget how to drive

Tell them they can't remember how to drive but don't want anyone to know. Now get them to teach you to drive.

Forget something important

Tell a good subject that on your cue they will have something very important to tell the whole world. Tell them that on your cue they will rush up to you, no matter where they are in the room, take your microphone and turn to tell the audience something important. The moment they turn they will totally forget what it was and return to their seat very confused.

Forget the alphabet

Tell them they can't remember the order of the letters in the alphabet. Tell them they can remember all the letters but have no idea on the order.

Forget the number three

Tell them they can't remember the number between two and four. Get them to rub it out in their minds. Say there never was a number between two and four and there never will be a number between two and four. Now tell them they know that all normal people have five digits on one hand and get them to count theirs, and yours.

Forget your address

Tell them they can't remember their address. They can recall what home looks like, but cannot remember the street name or the numbers.

Forget your gender

Tell them they can't remember what gender they are. Tell them they know they are male, female or 'other' and have to pick one.

Forget your nationality

Tell them they can't remember what country they are from.

Forget everything

Tell them they can't remember anything at all.

Fundraisers

This is ideal for a charity show. Tell them they are the world's greatest fundraisers and send them into the audience to collect money for the charity. Use the off mic control to tell one or two that if anyone is mean they will tell the whole world about it really loudly.

Game show genius

Tell your best verbal subject that they are the world's most famous game show genius. No matter what question you ask they will be able to answer it instantly.

Grand Prix

Get an audio track of motorcars racing and tell them that they are grand prix drivers. Funnier here if you tell them to cheat.

Gum Shoe

No, not 'detectives'. Tell them that they have chewing gum on their chairs. Tell them to clean it off their bottoms but it will then stick their fingers to their bottoms.

Hairdresser

Tell a guy he's a world famous hairdresser and to pick a lady from the audience and convince them that he knows what he is doing.

Hairy bodies

Tell all of the subjects that their entire body is becoming covered with hair, thick black hair and they find it sooo soft to stroke. For safety's sake, tell them no hair is growing…you know where.

Heckler

Send a loud subject to sit in the audience, preferably at the front. Have a chair put there for the purpose. Tell him that he is the world's worst heckler and that every time you touch your nose, he just has to heckle the hypnotist. Only do this if you can be really quick and funny when giving it back.

Hide away

Give them a fifty pound or dollar note. (Plain paper cut to approximate size.) Tell them to hide it where no one will find it.

Hippie

Tell them they are all becoming hippies from the sixties.

Hot and cold

Take them to a hot beach then immediately take them to a freezing cold room. Tell them they will begin to shake and shiver but that it's okay because there is a nice warm human body next to them.

Almost always they will put their arms around each other, if not just gently push them together.

I believe in fairies

Tell a subject that when they hear a particular word or phrase they will jump up and shout "I believe in fairies!" at the top of their voice. They will then know exactly what they have done and sit down feeling very silly. Other phrases that work are; the Russians are coming; Mummy, Mummy I need a wee, wee; Daddy, Daddy me done a poo, poo; yelling like Tarzan, (currently) Wasssup! And so on. Use these to trigger the others and get a chain reaction going.

I swear

Tell a guy he can't stop swearing and cussing. Every other word he says is too disgusting for the general public so, although he can think the word, he actually makes a bleep sound instead.

If I ruled the world

Tell them they all rule the world and they have totally outlandish ideas on how to make it better for themselves. I'd make a point of telling them that they are not racist or bigoted in anyway.

Insects

You are all at a picnic having a great time eating, drinking and laughing. On the count of three, insects are invading the picnic. 1, 2, 3. There are millions of insects all over your food and on you.

Interior Designer

Tell them they are the world's greatest interior designers and just hate the venue. Ask them what they will do with it. Use off mic.

control to get them to go way over the top. Or tell them that they are a fashion designer and they have to give advice to the audience.

Invisible hypnotist

Tell them that when they wake they will not be able to see you or the clothes you are wearing. They will be able to feel your touch, hear your voice and see anything you move but will not be able to see you. Tell them that no matter how scary this gets they will not leave the performing area. I sometimes add a flourish here by telling them that only my top half or legs are invisible. Often I do all three.

Jockeys

Tell them they are jockeys riding over the sticks in a big race, (Grand National in Britain). Tell them when they are coming to the jumps.

Kids' routines

One of the most popular routines you can do, and certainly one of the funniest, is to turn adults back into children. However a warning, do not regress them. You have no idea whether their childhood experiences were good or bad childhood. Always tell them they will *pretend* to be children.

Kids: Babies

Tell them you need their help. You are trying to find out where babies come from. Do they know?

Kids: Noisy and naughty

Tell all of the subjects they are back at school and six or seven years old, and that you are their teacher. They don't like you very much and whenever you turn your back they will be very noisy and naughty and will make silly faces at you. When you are looking at them they will be perfect angels.

Kids: Nursery rhymes

Tell them they are very young children and will each begin to say their favourite nursery rhyme over and over. Needs good use of the mic. here.

Kids: Teddy bears

Tell them it's bedtime and they are very tired but can't go to bed without their Teddy Bear. One of the grown ups in the audience has got it and they'll have to go and ask for it. The more tired they get the more they suck their thumbs etc.

Kids: Worst name

Tell them to tell you the worst name they can think of to call someone.

Kissy sticky

Tell a guy that when you wake him he is the world's greatest charmer. He always kisses the back of the ladies hands. The only problem is that when he does so his lips always stick to their hands until you release them. Wake him up and let him loose on the audience.

Lady of the night

Tell the guys they are ladies of the night and they are trying to attract the guys in the audience.

Laugh out loud

Tell them they find everything you say laugh out loud funny. Wake them and start to tell a really sad story. Always tell them they will not have an accident no matter how much they laugh; (there was this one time in Nottingham I'd rather not think about).

Liar

You are the world's biggest and worst liar. You lie and brag about absolutely everything and the more lies you tell the more outlandish they become.

Marching Band

Tell them they are the world's worst marching band, tell one of them that they are the drum major and give them a baton, broomstick will do, tell the rest of them to play their instruments and follow the drum major, badly. Play some music and send them into the audience.

Magician

Tell a strong subject they are the world's greatest Magician. Give them a cloth, tablecloth will do, and tell them that whatever or whomever they cover with the cloth will disappear when they shout abracadabra! Tell them they have an irresistible desire to 'disappear' everything.

Member

Tell the guys that their member (penis) has dropped off and rolled away.

Moan and groan

Tell them they have applied for jobs as voice-overs for a XXX rated movie, and that they are about to audition for you, the director.

Movies

Tell them they are at the movies watching the funniest film that was ever made, after a while tell them the film has changed to the saddest ever made. Describe the films to increase their reaction. To finish this routine, tell them they are watching the scariest movie they have ever seen.

Numb

Tell them different parts of their bodies have 'fallen asleep' and become totally numb.

Nutty Nurse

Tell them they are nurses and they have to give the people in the front row an injection. Tell them they won't take no for an answer.

Orchestra conductors

Play some music and tell them they are the world's greatest conductors.

Orchestra musicians

Play some music and tell them what instruments they are playing.

Orgasmic

Tell the girls that when you kiss them on the back of the hand they will have an orgasm. Tell the guys that when you shake their hands they will feel like they do when they orgasm but WILL NOT ACTUALLY HAVE ONE!

Party piece

Tell them that when you wake them they will perform their party piece. Tell them they can sing, dance, recite a poem, or tell a joke.

Raining

Tell them it's raining and they are getting soaked.

Red-Hot Chair

Tell them when you ask if they are warm enough, the chair they are sitting on becomes instantly very hot. (Tell them their skin will not blister or burn.) Tell them that when you say everything is cool they can sit down again.

Self-hypnosis

Tell one of the subjects they are the hypnotist. When you wake them and ask for a volunteer to hypnotise you that they will jump up and volunteer. Use your off mic. control here. Do exactly as they tell you but just at the point where they are about to put you under tell them to sleep. With practice the audience will never know.

Shadow Boxer

Tell them they are professional boxers, training. Get them to shadow box. Go up to the best and tell them they have a problem; the shadow keeps hitting them back.

Ship

Tell them they are on a ship and the sea is very rough, very rough. Do this standing and they wobble all over the place.

Shoe puppy

Tell them their shoe is a little puppy. Get them to pet it, play fetch, and take it for a walk. After a while tell them it has done what puppies do on the stage and that they have no poop bags with them and that there is a million pounds or dollar fine for fouling. (Even I have been surprised how some of them clean it up.)

Shout at the kids

Tell them they are parents of the world's most untidy kids who are sitting in the audience. Tell them that when they wake they will be shouting at the kids for being so untidy.

Sing song

Someone in the audience will have a birthday, on the day or close. Tell them that they will sing happy birthday to you at the tops of their voices when you wake them. As you walk along touch them on the shoulder saying, "You will sing in Chinese, you will sing in Portuguese", etc.

Slot machines

Tell them to be at a club or casino playing the slot machines. Put the money in and pull the arm and when you say 'Jackpot' they have just won a million.

Special cigars

Give them a large carrot each. Tell them they are the world's greatest connoisseurs of cigars and that this is the finest cigar ever made. Give them cigarette lighters and let them 'smoke' the cigars for a while. Then snap your fingers and tell them that the cigars are now the finest marijuana ever made. After getting a laugh, tell them the room is full of drugs squad police and that they have to hide them on their person.

Speeding

Tell them they have just been stopped by you, the traffic cop, for speeding well over the limit. Tell them they had better give a good excuse not to get a ticket.

Stars

Tell them they are all star celebrities. Interview some of them. Use the off mic. control to get a couple to be the same person and urge them to argue over who is the 'real' one.

Stiff

Make their arm go stiff and rigid so that it will not bend. Even funnier if you make their legs do the same and get them to try to walk. Use younger people for this as they may fall, otherwise do it sitting down for safety's sake.

Stink

Tell them there is a very bad smell coming from the person next to them. Tell them they can't get up and move away or move their chair. I compound this by 'blowing raspberries' on mic., telling them that every time they hear the sound it will get a million times worse. Always tell them they will not be ill or vomit here… just in case.

Stolen belly button

Tell them that when they wake they will notice that someone has stolen their belly button. Tell them to put their hands over the opening so that the air does not leak out. Even funnier if you get them to put their hands over someone else's 'hole'.

Strange Hands

Tell them that when you wake them they will notice they have the wrong hands – the person sitting next to them has theirs.

Strange shoes

Tell them that when they wake they will have on a strange pair of shoes. The only way to get comfortable is to take them off. Zap them back under and tell them that when they wake they will see their shoes and know that they have to wear them. The problem is that they don't remember how, or where on their body, shoes go.

Strong man

Use the largest male subject you have and use something very light; (the chair they are sitting on is perfect for this). Tell them to move the chair but also tell them that it weighs three tons and is impossible to move. Add comedy here by getting a child or very small woman from the audience or your subjects to move the chair for the poor guy.

Superhero

Tell a guy he is a super hero who can fly but someone must have done something to him because no matter how hard he tries, and he will try very hard, he will have trouble getting off the ground.

Telepathic hypnosis

Tell them that being relaxed makes them telepathic and that they can read your mind. Wake them and go to the corner of the stage. Tell them you will think the word sleep and when they receive that thought their eyes will close and they will go into an even deeper state.

Venue owners

Tell them they own the venue, bar, club, whatever. This doesn't work as well in a theatre situation. Tell them it is well past closing time and time for the customers to go home. Tell them to go around collecting empty glasses and shouting for everyone to go home. Always make sure they only remove empty glasses to the bar. Tell them they can be quite angry but not to physically 'throw' anyone out. (Do this and you will be very popular with the waiting and bar staff after the show).

Viagra

Tell the guys they have taken an overdose of Viagra and that the drug is kicking in. It is very embarrassing because their trousers are very tight.

Vibrator

Tell them that when they wake they will be a machine found in the home, a vacuum, washing machine, microwave. Now use your control and get one guy to be a vibrator. If he's really good get him to stand and turn him on to full 'thrust'.

We know what you did last night

Tell them all, it is now ten-thirty on the night before the show and that they are doing exactly what they were doing then. (For Pete's sake watch them closely in case you have to stop anyone fast.)

Weak

Give them a sheet of newspaper and tell them that no matter how hard they try they can't rip it.

Whirlwind

Tell them there is a whirlwind making their hands go round in a circle. Tell them it's getting faster and faster and that their hands will not stop turning. Tell them that when you snap your fingers the hands will begin to turn in the opposite direction.

Who would you like to talk to?

Give them a phone (I have one rigged with a microphone), and tell them they can phone anyone: real, fictional, alive or dead; God or Elvis, and tell them they can say anything they want to them. (Good excuse for some imaginative control here.) What about complaining to God about the weather? Go for it.

Windfall

Tell them there has been a bad road accident involving an armoured car and that the wind is blowing the money their way. They can keep any they collect but don't want anyone to know that they are doing it.

X-ray specs routine

Nearly all hypnotists use this routine, but by adding several other skits to it, it can become a major part of the show. Give them a pair of spectacles. (Buy some very cheap brightly coloured sunglasses and remove the lens.) Tell them that they are x-ray specs and that when they look through them they will be able to see every member of the opposite sex in the venue, naked. Nobody else knows what they can see so they can look as much as they like. Now separate out the men and 'sell' them the glasses for a fiver. Don't use the girls for this (the men are more likely to have cash with them). Remember who gave you what, as sometimes they will buy two or three pairs! At the end of the show you can give them this money back as a 'present' for being the best subjects. With the girls I get two guys from the audience to stand up and get the girls to give them points out of ten. It's a riot.

XXX Movie

Tell them they are watching an XXX movie. Tell all the girls they really like what's on the screen, tell the guys that they are prudes and think it's disgusting. Now tell them that they are the stars of the movie.

END

You've Read the Book

NOW see the DVD

from the Academy of Hypnotic Arts

In this unique training presentation you are taken from live masterclass footage, to the preparations for a show in front of an invited audience of hypnotists and guests, on to a specially edited version of that show with Jon's comments revealing the thought process and 'secret stuff' going on constantly in the background.

As in his book Deeper and Deeper the secrets of stage hypnosis, and in the LIVE School of Stage Hypnosis MasterClasses, the attention to safety, care and respect for the volunteers is paramount in the underlying philosophy of Jonathan Chase.

SSH

Secrets of Stage Hypnosis Masterclass

Who is this for?

This two day intensive masterclass is designed for the complete novice or indeed for the more experienced therapist seeking to extend their understanding and practical skills in the application and management of dynamic deep state hypnosis for fun or for presentation to groups.

Hypnosis for fun is safer than drugs, more informative than a stack of psychology books, faster than the speed of light and can even be lucrative for those with a desire to entertain and educate.

Results:

You will be able to present hypnosis to social groups or paying audiences from five to five thousand. You will be able to demonstrate the amazing results of deep trance states entertainingly, informatively and most importantly, safely. We have had people 'do their first show' the day they left this masterclass.

"The best fun I've ever had on a hypnosis course and this is the fifth I've done." Simon Rorke